A CHILD'S LIFE
of
MARY BAKER EDDY

MARY BAKER EDDY

*As she looked when preaching in
Boston in the years 1882 and 1883*

A CHILD'S LIFE

of

MARY BAKER EDDY

by

Ella H. Hay

Illustrated by
L. Franklin van Zelm

THE CHRISTIAN SCIENCE PUBLISHING SOCIETY
ONE, NORWAY STREET
BOSTON, MASSACHUSETTS, U. S. A.

Library of Congress Catalogue Card No. 42-50015

MJ

[Printed in U. S. A.]

FOREWORD

The author has long desired to give to children the appealing story of the life of Mary Baker Eddy, the Discoverer and Founder of Christian Science. This book is now offered as a simple record of a life that was beautiful from childhood.

The work of a biographer is to set down what the person about whom he is writing did and said; but the meaning of the story lies less in the words of the writer and more in the results of the person's lifework. A man's acts or works are his true biography. His works give meaning to his life story and make the story an inspiration to those who read it.

Only through understanding her words and works can one truly know Mrs. Eddy. Those numberless thousands in the four corners of the earth whose lives have been blessed through Christian Science know her in the way she would be known, as the humble servant of God.

The purpose of this biography is to acquaint children with the life of this remarkable and famous woman. It will fulfill its mission in keeping fresh in the minds of boys and girls the memory of the one who brought back Christian healing to mankind.

Most of the material for the story has been obtained from books already published on the life of Mary Baker Eddy. These books are: "Retrospection and Introspection," by Mary Baker Eddy; "The Life of Mary Baker Eddy," by Sibyl Wilbur; "Mary Baker Eddy: A Life Size Portrait," by Lyman P. Powell; "Christian Science and Its Discoverer," by E. Mary Ramsay; and "Historical Sketches," by Judge Clifford P. Smith. An expression of thanks is made to the authors of these books. The author is also grateful to the editor of the Bureau of History and Records of The Mother Church for the help of that office in checking certain historical information.

E. H. H.

CHAPTER 1

EVERYBODY wants to know something about the lives of those who are great and good as was Mary Baker Eddy, the Discoverer and Founder of Christian Science. She was a kind and gentle woman, a true follower of Christ Jesus, for she healed the sick and comforted those who were sad, just as he did. She gave us the key which explains the meaning of the Bible, making it so clear that even children can understand God and can heal the sick. People all over the world love and honor Mrs. Eddy for the good she has done; and as time goes on she will be honored more and more, because her life and work will be better understood.

She was a New England girl. Her father and mother lived on a farm in Bow among the hills of New Hampshire, one of the original thirteen states of the United States of America. Her father's name was Mark Baker, and her mother's name was Abigail. Mary was the youngest of six children, three boys and three girls. The names of her brothers and sisters were Samuel, Albert, George, Abigail, and Martha. Grandmother Baker, Mr. Baker's mother, also lived with the family when Mary was a child, so there were nine in all.

Mary's parents were intelligent and well educated. They were also earnest Christians. As a rule the entire family attended church services both morning and afternoon on Sunday. On weekdays they were equally faithful in serving God. Every morning they gathered together to read the Bible and to pray. Meals began with a prayer for God's blessing and ended with thanks to Him for His goodness. It was Mary's good fortune to have a home where thought was lifted often to God in prayer and praise.

Mr. and Mrs. Baker helped their children to build strong characters and to have good morals. Neither slang nor profanity was permitted in the household. Religion was often the topic of conversation, and ministers were frequent guests. The home was rich in friendliness and Christian fellowship. Long afterward Mrs. Eddy wrote of her childhood home as

2

"one with the open hand. The needy were ever welcome, and to the clergy were accorded special household privileges" (Retrospection and Introspection, p. 6).

Mary's mother often talked to her about God and read to her from the Bible. At bedtime she would sit by her little bed and tell her of God's love for His children. She would also impress on her such rules of behavior as, "Count that day lost whose setting sun finds no good done," and "Now remember child that a word that's flown is in your hearer's power and not your own." Mary never forgot her childhood bedtime hour, and the little hymn her mother sometimes sang to her:

> "How can I sleep while angels sing,
>   And hover o'er my bed;
> And clap their wings in joy to Him
>   Who is their glorious Head?"

Mary's father was a strict man, but he was also kind and generous. On holidays he used to load his wagon with chickens, apples, pumpkins, and other things raised on his farm and drive about the countryside sharing his goods with less fortunate neighbors. In one instance he permitted an invalid widow and her daughter to occupy a cottage he owned, free of rent.

He was a man of strong character, a pleasant man to meet, and he always treated others with kindness and respect. He was a leader in his community and was respected by his neighbors.

3

They often came to him for help in making out deeds and settling differences. Like most New Englanders, Mr. Baker was deeply interested in politics and education. He was careful to see that his children were well educated.

Mary's grandmother was as kind and good to her as her parents. She was a delicate child, and the dear old grandmother took her as her special charge, rocking the cradle with her foot as she knit away the hours in her chair by the fire.

As she grew older Mary loved to listen to her grandmother's stories of pioneer days and of brave ancestors who came to America seeking religious freedom. Once she asked her grandmother the question, "What is religion?" not dreaming that one day she would restore for mankind the religion of Christ Jesus.

John Baker was the first of her ancestors to come to America. He reached the shores of the New World shortly after the Pilgrims and settled near Boston. Several generations later Mary's great-grandfather traveled northward to New Hampshire for the purpose of surveying some land in a part of the colony that was claimed by Massachusetts. Finally he settled in Pembroke, one of the towns he surveyed. Pembroke is across the Merrimack River from Bow. Mary's mother, Abigail Ambrose, was born in Pembroke. She was the daughter of Deacon Ambrose, a religious man and a leader in the community. He gave the money for the first Congregational Church built in his town.

4

Mary liked to have her grandmother show her keepsakes. She had quite a store of them, some of which had been handed down from her grandmother and other relatives. Among the treasures were some newspapers, yellow with age, a little old book, and some manuscripts with verses and riddles written by Mary's great-grandmother. One of the newspapers contained a full account of the death and burial of George Washington, which occurred less than forty years before. Another keepsake was an old sword with a scabbard on which was engraved the name of the relative to whom it was given some five hundred years before by the Scottish patriot, Sir William Wallace. More than fifty years afterward Mrs. Eddy remembered her early interest in her grandmother's treasures and mentioned them in the story she wrote of her own life, entitled "Retrospection and Introspection."

The farm on which Mary was born was first settled by her grandfather, Joseph Baker. He was a prosperous farmer, the owner of considerable land, and the largest taxpayer in the Colony of New Hampshire. The farm was a large one of five hundred acres with the house on the top of the hill.

The house was not painted, as was customary in those days. It was large and comfortable, with a living room, guest chamber, kitchen, and pantries on the first floor and bedrooms above. Directly under the roof was a high garret. It was an old-fashioned New England garret, with spicy smelling herbs, pennyroyal, sassafras, catnip, and balsam buds hung in bundles under the low slanting rafters. Overhead were rows of home-cured meats, and below lay little piles of chestnuts, hazelnuts, and oilnuts (butternuts), gathered on crisp autumn days in the woods near by.

A carriage shed connecting the house and barn made the two buildings appear as one. This style of building is still common in rural New England, where winters are long and cold. Farmers are sometimes shut in by heavy snows for days at a time, and they need a covered passageway through which to reach their cattle.

Mary loved her childhood home. As a part of her wedding trip she drove from Concord to Bow to visit the scenes that  were ever dear to her. She loved the broad view with gentle slopes falling to the great Merrimack River. The brightness of river water could be seen on clear days from upper windows. In the far distance rose a faint line of mountains dimly reflecting the delicate tints of sunrise and sunset.

In front of the house was a garden with old-fashioned

6

flowers. Around the orchard was a broad stone wall overrun with wild roses and sweet briar and shaded with purple lilac. The children loved to play on the old wall; often they rested there, watching the nesting birds or the busy red squirrel, scampering down the stony pathway to his winter storehouse.

Back of the house was a clear little spring with sparkling water that cooled the milk and butter and supplied water for household use. This was a pleasant New England home, rather better than the average, for Mary's parents were prosperous.

CHAPTER 2

WE can understand Mary's life better by knowing something about the time and place in which she was born, and the people among whom she was reared. Her early life was different in many ways from the lives of modern boys and girls. She was born when the United States of America was quite young and before the time when the many inventions such as airplanes, automobiles, electric lights, and radios had a part in changing people's way of living.

Her birthday was July 16, 1821. The American War of Independence had been won less than fifty years before, and men of Mary's home state helped to win the victory. This war was fought because an English king refused the American colonists certain rights they were entitled to have. The colonists won the war and gained their independence. They were glad to be free and were ready to work together to establish a nation. Many years afterward Abraham Lincoln spoke of the government they formed as a "government of the people, by the people, for the people."

The people of New Hampshire were brave and hard-working. Early settlers established homes in the colony while it was still a wilderness with bears and other wild beasts roaming through the thick forests. Indians claimed the land as their own; and there was constant danger of uprisings among tribes unwilling to give their hunting ground to the white man.

It was no easy task to make a home in New Hampshire. The land was hilly and none too fertile. Before it could be plowed, heavy forests of oak and pine had to be cut and great numbers of stones picked from the ground. The stones were generally piled into broad fences surrounding fields and orchards. The early settlers worked from sunrise to sunset through the short summers raising food for their needs during the long winters; and winter hours found them hunting, trapping, mending and making tools to use when summer came again.

Mary lived several genera- tions after the first colonies were settled in New Hamp- shire. Even in her time the life of a hillside farmer was far from easy. There were  few of the conveniences of modern times. Houses were heated with fireplaces and stoves and lighted with candles. Kerosene lamps came later and so did matches. Candles and soap were made at home. Sugar was made from the sap of the maple tree.

9

White sugar, called "store sugar," was expensive and seldom used except by the well-to-do. Fruit and vegetables were dried instead of canned as in later years. Salt pork from the pork barrel in the cellar was the principal meat, especially in summer when there was no way of keeping fresh meat. Few people of early days thought of storing ice for summer use. Farm machinery was crude, and much of the labor of plowing, planting, and harvesting was done by hand.

Not being accustomed to doing much heavy work with our hands, we might think the lot of these pioneers a hard one, but they did not consider it so. They were brave and hard-working as their ancestors had been and were willing to work and ready to fight if they could obtain their rights in no other way. They knew what it meant to overcome difficulties through their own effort. The overcoming made them strong and gave them a feeling of independence. They were independent thinkers with a love of their country and a dream of what the land of opportunity would mean to their children and their children's children.

Everybody was interested in education, and book learning was valued highly in every home. Parents wanted their children to be well educated and prepared to take their places in the land of opportunity where the sons of rich and poor alike might rise to high positions. As early as 1769 New Hampshire had a college. This college was Dartmouth, located at Hanover. Common schools were built at the crossroads, and a number of cities and towns had academies. The common schools were much like grade schools of the present, and academies were somewhat like our public high schools. However academies were privately owned, with only a small part of their expense paid by public taxes. Pupils had to pay to attend academies, while the common schools were free. Children could receive a common school education with very little expense.

The Bible was a well-read book, for the people were very religious. Many of their ancestors had come to America seeking religious freedom. Later, if not permitted the freedom they thought they should have, they moved from colony to colony to find a place where they might worship God as they saw fit. Some of the early settlers of New Hampshire had moved north from Massachusetts mainly for religious reasons.

Mary first attended church in the little meeting house at Bow where her parents were members from the time of their marriage until the church was dissolved. Mary was then eight years old. Later, Mr. and Mrs. Baker became members of the First Congregational Church at Concord. This church was large and well attended, generally having good ministers. In the year of 1830 often as many as one thousand persons attended the services, coming from all directions, long distances, and many on foot. Walking was much more common than now. People thought little of traveling on foot five or six miles to attend church or to visit a friend.

When Mary was a little girl, the Sabbath was observed in the strict New England way, with no buying or selling nor any amusements. Early in the morning the family set out for church carrying a well-filled picnic basket, and not until milking time did they return. In her writings Mrs. Eddy mentions the Sabbath days of her childhood and the "grand old elm" that "flung its foliage in kindly shelter over" her "childhood's Sunday noons" (The First Church of Christ, Scientist, and Miscellany, p. 147). The children were expected to be quiet and serious. They spent the hours between the morning and afternoon services talking quietly as they sat under the spreading elm tree, perhaps scattering crumbs from their lunch for the nesting bluebird or bobolink.

From her early years Mary was deeply interested in religion and careful to keep the Sabbath day holy. She considered even letter writing too worldly for the Lord's Day, as may be seen from part of a letter to her close friend Augusta Holmes: "It is the Sabbath. I do not approve of writing letters on the Sabbath you know, but I could not find time ~~to~~ yesterday to write, & last evening I attended meeting.

"We have had a very interesting meeting to-day."

12

CHAPTER 3

THE part of New Hampshire in which Mary was born was a farming region during her girlhood. There were a few small cities, all built close to the large rivers. In early days most people settled near rivers so that they could get supplies brought from large cities by river boats and also send back whatever goods they had to sell, such as lumber, furs, and farm produce.

Transportation was quite difficult then and much slower than now. The first railroad to Concord was not completed until 1842. Mary was then past twenty. During her childhood, people traveled on boats and on horseback, or in carriages and stagecoaches. The latter were commonly used for long distances. Concord, a city about five miles from Mr. Baker's  home, was the beginning and end of several stagecoach lines. The coaches were drawn by four horses and could travel about eight miles an hour over turnpikes, as the best roads were called. These roads were owned by turnpike companies, and people had to pay to use them.

Side roads leading to main highways were very poor. Especially rough were the corduroy roads built over lowlands. A corduroy road was made from logs laid close together across the space marked out for the road. The logs for these roads were cut from the heavy forests that covered the hillsides. Corduroy roads were built over swampy land, and they made a practical road for the lowlands. Of course they were very rough. In one of her early letters to her brother, Mary joked about the roughness of roads and the means of transportation. She was always quick to see the funny side of things. The letter states: "I shall first enquire for your health, spirits, and the like of that, hopeing time sill continues to glide smoothly as in former years," and she adds, "it continues to do so with us only when we are obligeed to ride in a *wagon* and then it is rough."

Canal boats carried freight up the Merrimack River from Boston to cities and villages along the river. Boston was then as now the largest and most important city of New England. A canal from Boston to the Merrimack and smaller canals built around falls and rapids completed the waterway to Concord. Canal boats were either pushed by poles or pulled by horses. Paths were built beside the streams for use of animals towing the boats.

People who lived in Bow carried on most of their business

14

in Concord. Concord was the capital of the state and a city of nearly five thousand in 1840. A farm family of early days had comparatively little business in town. Most of the food was raised at home and prepared for use there as well. Butter and cheese were home products, and many farmers had their own treadmills for grinding corn and wheat. Clothing was made of wool from the home flocks. The wool was carded, spun, woven, and dyed at the fireside and also fashioned into garments. Men sometimes had "store clothes," but women's clothes were generally home-made.

Peddlers were a customary part of the life of the rural family. They were bearers of news and opinions as well as sellers of trinkets, beads, tinware, plated silver, spices, and notions and whatever else could be carried in a pack or on the back of a horse. They  were welcome guests. People stayed at home much more in early days than they do now; hence they looked forward to visits from these traveling salesmen, who were likely to bring more intimate news than the weekly newspaper and quite as much of it.

Some peddlers were venturesome and carefree, and may

have deserved their reputation for selling wooden nutmegs. This was meant to imply that they could not be trusted. Certainly many of them were upright men. Among them were students earning money for further schooling and educated men with a taste for travel and no better way of paying for it. The father of Louisa May Alcott, author of "Little Women," "Little Men," and a number of other good stories for boys and girls, was a peddler in his youth. Long afterward when he had become a well-known teacher and lecturer, he spoke encouragingly to Mrs. Eddy of the future of Christian Science. His encouraging words came at a time when as yet few well-known persons felt that her religion would prosper. Abraham Lincoln also tried peddling for a brief period, selling twenty dollars' worth of notions to settlers he passed on the journey with his father's family from Indiana to Illinois. No doubt Mary had many contacts with peddlers. Part of one of her mother's letters reads, "Your pocket handkerchief peddler called."

Farmers who lived around Concord had reasons for going to town even though little food or clothing was purchased. A city directory of Concord published in 1830 lists the services that people in and near the city could obtain in town. Among the business and professional establishments listed in the directory are three apothecaries (druggists), four milliners, three painters, three tanners, two boatbuilders, seven cordwains (shoemakers), five blacksmiths, three wheelwrights, one truck-man, five tailors, and one music teacher. It seems strange to us that a city of five thousand should have only one music teacher and only one truckman. Concord had more blacksmiths, wheelwrights, and boatbuilders than most cities of the same size have today, and three tanners would seem quite a number for a small city now. In the early days farmers did considerable trapping and hunting. Sometimes the skins were tanned at home; and sometimes they were prepared for use by tanners. Probably the farmers near Concord carried many of the skins to town to be tanned. The boatbuilders, druggists, wheel-wrights, milliners, and tailors served the farmers as well as the city people, and even the town blacksmith may have helped the country folk.

People who lived in Bow went to Concord for their mail, at least until 1832, when the first post office in Bow was established. The new post office was in charge of a private postmaster who appointed a helper to fetch the mail from Concord. A fee was charged for receiving as well as for send-ing mail. Postage stamps were not in use until 1847.

Letter writing had an important part in the family life of Mary's home. Mary carried on a correspondence with friends and cousins as well as with her brothers, all of whom were

17

away from home at different times during her girlhood. Both Samuel and Albert were gone much of the time. Samuel carried on a contracting business in Boston. He was married when Mary was only ten. Albert, the most scholarly of the boys, attended Dartmouth College. After his graduation he studied and also practiced law in Hillsborough. For a time he shared the law office of Franklin Pierce, who later became President of the United States. Some of Mary's early letters were written to her schoolmate Augusta Holmes. She wrote regularly for a number of years to her cousin Hildreth Smith, and frequently to a close friend, Martha Rand, who later married George Baker and became Mary's sister-in-law.

A number of Mary's letters as well as some written by other members of the family have been saved. These give interesting glimpses of the family life. In one of her letters to Mary when she was married and living in the South, Mrs. Baker describes the home during an evening:

"Martha is much engaged in sewing but cannot lay out her work to good advantage, having *new patterns*. We wish you were here to assist her. . . . Dear Mahala sits braiding, your father sits reading, you know I am always at work. We miss your good cheer." "Mahala" was Mahala Sanborn, the daughter of a blacksmith of Tilton. She was sometimes employed by Mr. Baker to help with the housework. Much of

18

the work of the house and farm was done by members of the family; however, farm hands and household help were employed to assist.

Mary's letters were long and many, considering the expense of letter writing and the difficulty in sending them. Paper was expensive and envelopes unknown. The paper was folded over and sealed with wax. The cost of sending a letter consisting of one piece of paper, not going over thirty miles, was six cents; not going over eighty miles, was ten cents. For longer distances the cost ranged from ten cents to twenty-five cents. These rates do not seem high, considering the slow and toilsome transportation of early days. However, they seemed high to people living then. Twenty-five cents could buy more in Mary's time than in later years; hence it seemed like more money. Both wages and prices were low then as compared with a century later. Money was scarce, and business was carried on largely by trading.

To lessen the expense of letter writing, people often sent their messages by friends, acquaintances, or peddlers. In one of her early letters to her brother George, Mary wrote, "As I have an opportunity of sending you a letter . . . without putting you to that expense which any intelligence I could communicate would but ill repay I improve it with pleasure." A letter to Mary from her brother Albert begins in almost the same way: "I have an opportunity of sending a letter by a friend of mine, . . . who is going to Sanbornton with the intention of attending the academy."

"Sanbornton" was Sanbornton Bridge, a town near which Mr. Baker moved when Mary was fifteen. The town was renamed in 1869 and is now called Tilton.

CHAPTER 4

MARY was a beautiful child, with deep blue eyes, fair skin, and chestnut curls that hung over her shoulders. She grew into an attractive young maiden and a lovely woman. One of her cousins describes her at eighteen as a "frail, fair young maiden with transparent skin and brilliant blue eyes, cheerful, hopeful, and enthusiastic."

Her remarkable spirituality became evident when she was a child. She loved the Bible and knew its characters so well that they seemed like friends. Like Daniel, whose story she loved to hear, Mary prayed often. For a long time she prayed seven times a day, and for each prayer placed a mark on the woodshed door. Mary wrote down some of the prayers and sometimes read them over to see what progress she had made.

A number of unusual experiences occurred in her life while she was still quite young. One was at the age of eight. During one year she repeatedly heard a voice calling her by name. At first she thought it was her mother calling and went to ask what she wanted. Her mother always replied, "Nothing, child! What do you mean?" Then Mary would say, "Mother, who

21

did call me? I heard somebody call *Mary,* three times!" (Retrospection and Introspection, p. 8.) This continued until she grew discouraged and ceased heeding the call.

Once the call came when her cousin, Mehitable Huntoon, was visiting her. It was clear and distinct, and even Mehitable heard it. Mary paid no attention until her cousin asked why she didn't answer her mother. Then she went to her mother, but found as before that she had not called.

When Mrs. Baker learned that Mehitable too had heard the voice, she laid aside her work and returned with Mary to the room where the children had been playing. Taking Mehitable aside, she questioned her, asking if she really did hear Mary's name called. The child replied that she had heard the voice distinctly calling Mary's name.

To help her little daughter understand this unusual experience, Mrs. Baker read her the story of the child Samuel and bade her reply as he did when the voice was heard again, "Speak, Lord; for Thy servant heareth." The call came again, but Mary was afraid and did not answer. Afterward she wept bitterly at her failure and promised next time to do as her mother had suggested. She kept her promise, and the next time *did* answer ". . . in the words of Samuel, but never again to the material senses was that mysterious call repeated." (Retrospection and Introspection, p. 9.)

22

At the age of twelve she had an unusual religious experience. She was eager to become a member of the church of which her parents had long been members, but could not agree with the belief of the church that pictured God as a god of revenge and anger. Both her father and the minister tried to convince her that she must accept the beliefs of the church; but Mary would not agree with what she felt was wrong. She was so worried over the problem that she became ill with a fever, and a doctor was called. Her mother comforted her and bade her lean on God's love and find peace. So Mary prayed; and, to use her own words, ". . . a soft glow of ineffable joy came over me. The fever was gone, and I rose and dressed myself, in a normal condition of health. Mother saw this, and was glad. The physician marvelled. . . ." (Retrospection and Introspection, p. 13.)

Not long after this experience she made a statement of her beliefs about God which was accepted by the church in spite of her refusal to agree with the stern thought of God. Five years later, when seventeen, she became a member of the First Congregational Church in Tilton.

Mary was a kind and generous child, always ready to share what she had with others. Her sweetmeats, her toys, her little store of nuts gathered in the pastures—all these she shared freely. Others might gather for themselves, looking forward to frosty evenings about the cheery fire with chestnuts snapping and sputtering on the hearth; but Mary's gathering was primarily for others.

Although she liked to sit alone in school, she shared her seat with a timid child who needed a friend. More than once  she gave her own warm scarfs and mittens to needy children who came to school with purple hands and stinging ears. It was natural for her to think of others more than of herself. A person who knew her well in later years said he had never known so unselfish an individual.

She used to help one of her father's chore boys prepare his Sunday school lessons. He was a good boy, but had not gone to school and could not read. Both Mary and her father wanted him to go to Sunday school; but he was bashful about it because he could not repeat Scriptural verses like other children. Mary often read to him from the Bible and repeated verses to him; but he would forget them as soon as she had finished. So she adopted the plan of reading a verse to him and then repeating it over and over until he could say it. In this way he learned the verses and could recite them in Sunday school.

24

Even when a child Mary showed remarkable courage in doing what she thought was right and in protecting others. In school she took the part of younger children when they were teased by the older ones. Once she faced an insane man who entered the yard of the academy she was attending. He was swinging a large club, and the children ran away terrified, all but Mary. She spoke to the sick man gently, asking him to leave the yard. He became quiet at once. The club fell to his side, and he walked through the gate to the street. The following Sunday he appeared at church and stood beside her during the singing. Later he went away quietly with those who came to care for him.

Mary disliked quarreling and sometimes acted as peacemaker among her brothers and sisters and playmates. In one instance she made peace between two quarreling farmers who came to her father for help in settling a difference. Mr. Baker was often called upon to settle disputes and sometimes to argue cases in court. Once he argued a case in which Mr. Franklin Pierce, future President of the United States, was opposing counsel. Mr. Baker presented a good argument and won the case against the well-known and able lawyer. Mr. Pierce bowed and congratulated him. No doubt he was surprised that one who was not a student of law could present such a fine argument.

Mary happened to be in the room when the two quarreling farmers came in. She was disturbed by their loud voices and  came from her corner. Facing one of them she said quietly, "Mr. Bartlett, why do you articulate so vociferously?" Her manner and words seemed very old for a child, and the men were amused. They forgot their anger, and the difference was soon settled. Mr. Baker always said, "Mary settled that quarrel."

She seldom used such big words as those spoken to Mr. Bartlett. Her early letters show that she expressed herself in simple language, easy to understand. However, she always knew a great many words. She used eighteen thousand in her writings on Christian Science. This unusual number places her second only to the great poet, Shakespeare, in the number of words used by those who have written in the English language.

She was always adding new words to her vocabulary by reading and thinking about what she read, also by listening to her elders. Ministers often visited in the home, and Mr. Baker used to talk with them about religion. Young as she was, Mary liked to listen to their talks, and sometimes she joined in. Long afterward she listed among her great blessings her early association with well-known ministers. During her childhood she had the opportunity of hearing the sermons of several able ministers. These sermons made a lasting impression on her, because she was interested in spiritual things.

We must not think that Mary was so deeply concerned with religion that she had no fun. She was a very happy child and enjoyed the companionship of her brothers and sisters and friends. As she grew older, she attended parties and weddings and other social gatherings. She frequently mentioned good times in her early letters. At sixteen, writing to her brother George, she speaks of a "gentleman . . . from Boston, . . . a *perfect complet gentleman,*" adding, "*I met him a number of times at parties last* winter . . . I have since then attended a wedding with a Mr. Bartlett he was goomsman and I bridsmaid; we had a fine time I assure you."

In another letter to George she tells of "a party of young Ladies at Miss Hayes," adding, "she was truly sorry our Brother from Conn. was not there, but she is soon to be married."

Mary had several vacations during her girlhood and traveled what was then considered a long distance. One trip was to Boston, a distance of nearly one hundred miles southward, and another to the White Mountains, about eighty miles northward. The following is part of a long and interesting letter written to her brother from Haverhill, where she was visiting

Augusta. Haverhill was about fifty miles, a day's stagecoach journey, from Tilton.

"My dear Brother:

"Since I left you I have made it a religious duty to obey you in *all things*. And today, according to promise, write you the order of exercises since Wednesday—I reached here about 6 o'clock P.M. was the only passenger inside, and such a *sky-rocket* adventure I never had; some times I really thought I was at least *midway* betwen heaven and earth, till the driver's shrill whistle, or a more tolerable road would restore my senses; Mr. Hale is the very most polite good natured driver in the *whole world* (As *I have seen it all*) and was very kind to me on your account I suppose—You cannot know how *lame* and unwell I felt *yesterday;* . . . Augusta and *all* want me to stay here until commencement And then attend with them, but there is so much to excite me here, and such a teazing etiquette in this vill. it is not best for my health And I go to L. to-night—*God bless you*

"Mary"

CHAPTER 5

MARY spoke of the condition of her health more than once in her early letters. She was not strong, and she was often ill both when a child and in later years until she was restored to health through Christian Science. Sickness kept her out of school much of the time and also interfered with her good times.

Her first schooldays were spent in the one-room building on the road to Concord. Mary was a natural student, always a lover of books. When only a little girl she expected to write a book some day. Before she was of school age, her sisters sometimes took her to school with them to visit.

During the lunch hour they would set her on the table top and ask, "Mary, what are you going to do when you grow up?" And she would reply, "I will write a book."

The schoolhouse was only a mile from home, so the Baker girls walked most of the time, carrying their lunches. Their brothers had finished the work of the country school before Mary was old enough to enter. Samuel was already engaged in business, and Albert was in college. George was still at home. In bad weather he drove his sisters in the "democrat wagon" or one-horse shay and brought them home again.

The schools of New Hampshire were better than many early schools. Country school buildings had only one room, up to thirty feet in length and about twenty feet wide. The furnishings were crude. In the middle of the room was a stove, and around it were benches for the children. The higher benches were for older children, and the lower ones in front for the "infants," as primary children were called. In one corner was a water bucket with a dipper which the children all used, and in another corner was the teacher's desk with inkstands, goosequills, leaden plummets for ruling paper, and a birch rod to punish the mischief-maker and to prod the slow learner.

The teachers were often good, although wages were low. Twelve dollars a month and keep was a common wage. "Keep" meant that the teacher had no expense for board and room, since the parents of school children took turns "keeping" him in their homes.

There were few books in the early school. The texts were a reader, grammar, speller, and the New Testament. Noah

30

Webster's speller was in common use. It sold into millions of copies. Readers were ungraded until 1840. This means that in the school Mary attended "infants" learned to read from books that were better suited to much older children.

Early schools were not so good as modern schools, yet the children were interested in learning. It was something of a distinction to be a good reader when many of their parents were not. School hours were spent repeating the A B C's, studying long lists of spelling words and rules of grammar, and learning verses from the Bible. The texts were studied from beginning to end and the lessons recited to the teacher.

A few pictures helped to hold the children's interest. The pictures were in black and white and were made from woodcuts. They were used to illustrate fables. Fables are untrue stories that are made up to teach a lesson. Among the fables used in early readers were, "The Maid Who Spilled the Milk," "The Dog in the Manger," "The Hare and the Tortoise," and "The Woman Who Counted Her Chickens Before They Were Hatched." The lesson to be taught by the story was always printed at the end and was considered the most important part of the story. Everything read in school pointed out the wisdom of doing right and the folly of doing wrong.

Rhymes were sometimes used in teaching numbers, and these never failed to interest the children even when the solution was difficult. Here is an example of one of the teaching helps used by early teachers:

"A gentleman a chaise did buy,
   A horse and harness too;
They cost the sum of threescore pounds,
   Upon my word 'tis true.
The harness came to half th' horse,
   The horse twice of the chaise;
And if you find the price of them,
   Take them and go your ways."

(From "The Schoolmaster's Assistant," by Thomas Dilworth)

Mary learned to read from the Bible and from Lindley Murray's Reader. Long afterward she recalled reading the Scriptures at school and said, "My earliest best impressions of Truth, which could come at that date, were rec'd from reading the New Testament every morning at school."

Her reader was a little book, bound in brown calf, with very fine print and no pictures. Children of early days did not have colorful books with large print and good illustrations such as are used now. Mary and many other young people liked the reader, although it was not attractive.

The book was difficult to read. The very first page begins with "Rules and Observations for assisting Children to read with Propriety." On one page we find: "The acquisition of knowledge is one of the most honourable occupations of youth."

"Diligence, industry, and proper improvement of time, are material duties of the young." The pages are filled with such wise sayings as, "Disappointments and distress are often blessings in disguise," and "Whatever purifies, fortifies also the heart."

The difficulty of the little brown book did not disturb Mary, for she learned easily. At the age of ten she was as familiar with her Lindley Murray as with her Westminster Catechism, and the latter she had to repeat every Sunday. Her memory was remarkable, and she gained book knowledge with little effort. In later years she told one of her secretaries that when a little girl she could remember whatever she read and never forgot anything. She used to be, as she said, "prompter for the entire family, my father and all of them."

She did not go to the country school long, for it soon was seen that school attendance was telling on her health. A doctor whom her father consulted advised keeping her at home and away from books, and encouraged her to exercise in the fresh air and sunshine. So Mary was left free to wander with the wind among the wild flowers she loved and to make friends with the trees and with the birds in their branches.

For several years her education went on at home. Different members of the family helped her, each in his own way. She had excellent tutors, several able ministers, and her brother Albert, who taught her during his vacations from college.

Mary's mother was one of her best teachers and probably did more than any other to prepare her for her lifework as Discoverer and Founder of Christian Science. Mrs. Baker was well educated and read good books; also the newspapers and magazines of the day. In her time women were considered less intelligent than men. They were granted few rights by law. Not until after 1830 were they allowed to speak in public. Most people felt that women should be interested only in the home, church, and family. In spite of this feeling, Mrs. Baker had wide interests. She was highly respected in her community because of her strong character and good deeds. Her opinions were valued by educated men who knew her.

She was a capable housewife and taught her daughters to be good housekeepers, thrifty and hard-working. Mary learned the household arts and crafts, how to weave, knit, sew, and cook, and how to manage a home with care and wisdom. Sewing was a difficult task in early days when women's clothes were of many folds, and patterns generally homemade. Mary found her knowledge of sewing very useful. She was always well dressed, because she knew how to make the best use of both

34

time and money. She had good taste and knew what to wear and how to wear it.

Many years after her childhood days, when lecturing in Boston, she wore a rich-looking purple dress that appeared to be velvet. A man in the audience who had come to mock rather than to hear the sermon questioned why she wore such expensive clothes when preaching Christianity. As nearly as can be remembered, Mary replied, "There are ladies here I presume with much more expensive dresses on, as this is velveteen, thirty-six inches wide, and only one dollar per yard." She might have added that she sometimes made her own dresses and even her bonnets, because she felt the importance of being well dressed and could not afford to hire the work done.

In later years Mary liked to recall her mother's teaching. Once she told a friend about an early lesson in thrift. It happened one evening when the family was gathered around the fire with Mr. Baker reading and Mrs. Baker sewing, while the children shelled corn for the chickens, as they often did. While shelling a big yellow ear Mary dropped a grain from her lap, and with her little foot pushed it toward the open grate. Her mother said, "Mary, get down and pick up that corn."

Mary answered, "Oh! Mother, it is only one grain."

"Never mind," said her mother, "it will help to make a meal for a little chick."

At no time did Mary neglect her studies. She was always fond of books and never left them alone for long. When in school she used to carry her reader home at night and sometimes take it to bed with her. From her childhood she read and studied difficult books. She also read the newspapers, reading not only for herself but for the family as well. Sometimes at night when her father sat reading the news, she would call from her bed, "Father, I know what you are doing: you are reading the newspaper."

He would reply, "Hush, child, and go to sleep."

Then she would say, "I'll read it to you." Of course, she did not know all the words, but her father was satisfied.

When only nine years old she had read Young's "Night Thoughts." And she understood it—so she told her brother Albert, who was home on his first vacation from Dartmouth. She also confided in him her plan to write a book when she grew up, adding that she must have a good education to do it. "I must be as great a scholar as you or Mr. Franklin Pierce," she said.

Few girls of Mary's time expected a higher education, and there was little opportunity to obtain such learning except through tutors. Most people considered college education for women both foolish and unnecessary. In the entire United States, Oberlin was the only college open to both boys and girls. Mount Holyoke, the first college for women, was established when Mary was past sixteen.

Albert was pleased with his little sister's interest in learning. He advised her to study Latin and her Lindley Murray; and he promised to help her during his vacations. He kept his promise, and they studied together each summer, reading Latin, Hebrew, and Greek, as well as philosophy and natural science. These seem difficult subjects for a child, but Mary could learn them. She was eleven years younger than Albert, but she seemed nearer his age. They were close companions, as may be seen from a letter introducing a friend, which he wrote her during her sixteenth year:

"I take great pleasure in introducing him to your acquaintance. You will find him a sterling fellow, a little enthusiastick, but none of Sol Wilson about him. What is that poor devil doing? I hope you treat him as he deserves, with entire neglect." Continuing the letter Albert describes the friend he is introducing as a "very close student . . . as much given to *discursive talking* as yourself, though he has not quite so much poetry at his command. . . .

Albert had a deep influence on Mary's life. He was an unusual character and a brilliant scholar, considered by his college as one of its finest students. He was always ready to work for what he thought was right. When a member of the New

Hampshire State Legislature he worked for better laws and opposed unfair practices such as imprisonment for debt. He was a pioneer in the temperance work of his state. Temperance meant refusing any drink that contained alcohol. For nearly one hundred years after the early beginning of temperance work, in which Albert had an important part, temperance workers all over the country were organized. They had meetings and sent out lecturers and worked together to reform those who drank and to encourage people to promise that they would not drink any alcoholic drink.

We find a glimpse of Albert's character in a part of a letter to his brother George: "My rule is *to do the best I can,* and whatever happens, . . . to submit cheerfully. . . . Now apply this rule. Have you done all you could do? If so, be content with the event; if not, learn by the past how to regulate the future." Mary was very fond of Albert. She once wrote he "was, next to my mother, the very dearest of my kindred" (Retrospection and Introspection, p. 6).

Her cousin, Hildreth Smith, was another with whom she studied in her early years. They were about the same age and used to like to read together and discuss poetry and philosophy. They often recited verses to each other, sometimes reciting those Mary herself had written. In later years Mr. Smith became a well-known writer and teacher. He spoke of her with deep

38

affection and respect, saying: "I have known the Rev. Mary Baker Eddy from childhood. She is my first cousin. Her mother was my mother's younger sister. She was always a beloved visitor in our home. . . . Her brother Albert was one of the ablest lawyers of New Hampshire; but Mary was deemed the most scholarly member of her family. She has always held a sacred place in my heart."

CHAPTER 6

IN the spring of 1836, a few months before Mary's fifteenth
birthday, her father moved from his farm in Bow, New
Hampshire, to another farm twenty-two miles northward,
in the same state. The new home was one mile out of
Tilton. Shortly after settling, Mary enrolled in school once
more. Late that summer one of her brothers wrote to another,
"Mary has attended school all summer, and is quite as well as
could be expected." The Sanbornton Academy was scarcely a
mile down the highway that ran past her father's farm and
into Tilton. It was open to both boys and girls. There had
been no academy within easy walking distance of her home in
Bow. No doubt she was glad to be so near a good school and
welcomed the opportunity to continue her studies with young
folks of her own age and interests.

Tilton was smaller than Concord, numbering less than
three thousand in 1830. It was a pleasant place in which to
live, having naturally beautiful surroundings and a number of
other advantages. Among the advantages were good schools,
three churches, a publisher of books, and a local newspaper.
The town was a manufacturing center and had a fast-growing

cloth mill owned by Alexander H. Tilton. Mr. Tilton was a prominent young business man who later became the husband of Mary's sister, Abigail.

Mary lived with her parents in their home at the edge of Tilton for nearly twelve years, except for a short time after her marriage to Major Glover. During the twelve years between 1836 and 1848 she completed her schooling, married, and went with her husband to the South, and later returned in sickness and sorrow to the loving care of her parents. She continued to live with them until after the death of her mother.

Like the house in which she was born, the new home was on the top of a hill. The view was much the same as from the hilltop in Bow. It was a broad and inspiring view of gentle slopes, wide valleys, and misty mountains outlined more clearly against the sky. Tilton was twenty miles nearer the White Mountains than Bow. A mile below the farm ran the swift Winnepesaukee River, rushing its supply of mountain water to feed the great Merrimack. Just beyond the city lay the beautiful Silver Lake, and a little farther away the larger lakes, Winnesquam and Winnepesaukee. The latter is the lake to which Mrs. Eddy referred when she spoke of the Indians calling "a certain beautiful lake 'the smile of the Great Spirit'" (Science and Health with Key to the Scriptures, p. 477).

The many bodies of water in and around Tilton added to

the beauty of the surroundings and furnished fun for the young people both in winter and summer. However, from early days pupils of the academy were forbidden to engage in sports "in and around the river," according to the catalogue of Sanbornton Academy.

The Bakers' home seemed less like a country home in Tilton than in Bow. The farm was much the same, with its fields of grain, its orchard surrounded by the broad stone wall, and its herds and flocks grazing on hillside and pasture. But living

so near town the family was a part of the town community rather than of the surrounding country. A mile was a short distance to walk, and the home became a center of social gatherings for young people of Tilton.

Mr. and Mrs. Baker joined the First Congregational Church, and Mr. Baker became the superintendent of the Sunday school. Mary united with the same church and taught in the Sunday school. She must have made a pleasing picture in the old meetinghouse with her delicate beauty and gentle grace. One of her Sunday school pupils long afterward wrote, "I would learn a few verses from the Bible, and after repeating them to her, she would explain them to me. She was very pretty to look at; her cheeks very red, her hair was brown curls, she had beautiful eyes. She wore a cape of moire silk. . . . Her bonnet was white straw and had a pink rose in each side, with her curls she was just lovely."

Many who knew her in later years spoke of her beauty and grace, and few failed to mention her lovely eyes. There were many also who spoke of the inward light that seemed to shine through her face, making one feel the desire to be loving and good. She was always so tender and kind that her very presence was a blessing.

We do not know exactly how long Mary was enrolled in the different academies she attended. We do know, however, that she attended the Holmes Academy at Plymouth when seventeen. While in this school she formed a close friendship with Augusta Holmes, to whom many of her early letters were written. In a catalogue of the Sanbornton Academy, her name is among the students for three terms ending November 21, 1842. She was then past twenty-one, an age at which few girls of her time were interested in schooling. In the same catalogue the name, Mark Baker, Esquire, appears as one of the trustees.

When not in school she often studied under tutors. One of her tutors was the Reverend Enoch Corser, pastor of the First Congregational Church of Tilton. He was the pastor who first received Mary into communion in the church. He was a well-educated man and so capable that he tutored his son through his first two years of college work, enabling him to enter as a junior. Mary's unusual ability interested the minister. He used to like to talk with her and listen to her poems. Often they talked about deep subjects, which his son long afterward said were too deep for him.

She must have inspired the fine old churchman and perhaps led him to a greater faith in the all-loving Father. Once he said to her, "Mary, your poetry goes beyond my theology, why should I preach to you!" Many years later his son recalled Mary's unusual gift of expression and her vocabulary which was, he said, far larger than that of most girls of her time. He said that his father once spoke of her as "bright, good, and pure," adding: "I never before had a pupil with such depth and independence of thought. She has some great future, mark that. She is an intellectual and spiritual genius."

Mary was growing in ability to express herself in writing. She was already known as a promising young poetess. One of her teachers in the academy in Tilton encouraged her to use her talent, saying, "You will some day be a distinguished

44

author." While she was still a young girl some of her poems were printed in newspapers and magazines, and later a number of them were reprinted in a collection entitled, "Gems for You."

Her letters were her main prose compositions during her early years. Her thought ran more naturally to poetry than to prose. To use her own words, "Poetry suited my emotions better than prose." (Retrospection and Introspection, p. 11.) The poetic feeling found in much of her prose bears out her statement. For example, a letter to Augusta begins, "Your letter (or  rather treasure) received but two days since, came like the morn's refreshing dew to the early flower, reviving the thirsty hope of joy that hath *long, too long,* been defered."

Mary's early letters give an interesting picture of her girl-hood. To Augusta she writes of books, of nature, and of fun, with bits of harmless gossip such as girls like to write to one another. Her letters show a growing interest in books. One begins, "My dear Augusta, Have you Surwalt's grammar? If so, would you do me the favour to loan it to me for a short time? I am told it is easier than Levizac's—at least if it is not I shall have *horrors* worse than last evening—*after you left* are you well, and did you return safely? but answering echo must reply to this."

45

Even an invitation to a party was likely to include a mention of books. For example, when inviting Augusta she adds the following long postscript to a very short letter: "You will please to bring along with you that favourite book of mine,— entitled, *Forget me not* I have not had an opportunity to send to Concord for one yet."

Her letters show an interest in religion. To comfort Augusta after the death of her father she writes: "Have you not been enabled in this time of sorrow and distress to cast all your care upon Him who careth for us? I believe you once told me that you had a hope in Christ. If so you will not need to turn to the world for comfort, and for balm for your wounded heart, for in Christ 'all fulness dwells.' "

Sometimes she moralizes as in the following, also to Augusta, ". . . the friendship which has existed between us, is founded upon a basis too solid to be shaken by trifles. How many friendships (so-called, but sadly miscalled) have such a foundation that a mere word is sufficient to dissolve them forever. But I *hope* such will not be the case with us. If we each possess a forgiving spirit, much pain may be spared us." Again she writes, "I think if every one would be cautious in reporting flying stories, a great deal less of falsehood would be spoken."

46

CHAPTER 7

A T the age of twenty-two Mary became the wife of George Washington Glover, a building contractor of South Carolina, who formerly lived in Concord. He was a brother-in-law of Samuel Baker and had learned the first steps in the building trade with him.

Many years afterward Mrs. Eddy told one of her secretaries about her early meetings with her future husband. The first time was at the age of ten. ". . . it was at the marriage of her brother, Samuel Dow Baker to Maj. Glover's sister, Eliza Ann Glover, and he took her on his knee and asked her how old she was. She told him ten years old. He said he would come in exactly five years, and then said jokingly that he would make her his little wife; whereupon she jumped off his knee and hid herself. He came back again in exactly five years, when her sister Abigail married Alexander Tilton, . . . she expected to see him at this wedding. The third time was at the age of twenty-two in Tilton. She was going along the street and thought it was her brother George, so she slapped him on the back and said, 'Oh, you're dressed up.' " When he looked around she saw to her shame that it was Major Glover.

They were married in December, soon after this third meeting, in the home of her parents near Tilton. The house was gay and festive for the happy event, and guests came from far and near. Of both relatives and friends the Bakers had many. All of Mary's brothers and sisters were present except Albert. Death had ended his promising career a few years before. At the time he was in line for the important service to his country of United States Congressman from New Hampshire.

Samuel and his wife came up from Boston for the wedding. The new railroad to Concord was completed the year before, and the journey that far could be made in less than half a day.

The remainder of the way to Tilton took nearly as long by stagecoach. Martha and Abigail were both present with their husbands. Abigail had been married six years; and Martha was now the wife of Luther C. Pilsbury, a state warden. She made her home in Concord. George was still unmarried and living at home.

The marriage ceremony was performed by the Reverend Corban Curtice, Mary's beloved pastor. She was an attractive, happy bride, rich in the good wishes of her friends and relatives. She was well prepared to build a happy Christian home such as the one in which it was her good fortune to be reared.

Ever loving and thoughtful of others, one of her last acts on her wedding day before departing with her husband for Charleston, South Carolina, was to go with her mother to the home of a neighbor to visit a sick child.

After a day in Concord and Bow, Mr. and Mrs. Glover traveled to Boston, where they set sail on the journey of nearly one thousand miles to their new home in the South. Before they were far out of the harbor the ship ran into heavy weather, and soon it was tossing about on the waves. On Christmas Day the storm became very severe. The passengers were frightened, and even the captain was uneasy. As had always been her way when in trouble, Mary turned to God in prayer. She and her husband knelt on the floor of the cabin and prayed. Before

long the sea was calm again, and all were safe. The captain was surprised at the sudden change in the weather and said that a miracle had taken place.

Now that her home was in the South, Mary's attention was held by the problem of slavery. From childhood she had heard discussions of the subject. Lindley Murray's Reader, which she knew from cover to cover, took a stout stand against slavery and pointed out the cruelty of holding man in bondage. Mr. Baker considered it a sin for one man to own another, and so did many other New Englanders.

50

Charleston was in the midst of the old South. Huge plantations worked by slaves surrounded the city. Mrs. Glover used to drive through the country with her husband, and once she passed a chapel where negroes were worshiping. She heard them express "their trust in God and Jesus Christ their only Saviour from slavery." She was touched by their simple faith and longed to help them.

Convinced that slavery was wrong, she became an active defender of the colored man. It was never Mary's way to permit a wrong to continue unchallenged. Her first step was urging her husband to free the slaves he owned. Mr. Glover had been born and reared in the North, and he also was opposed to slavery. But he had lived three years in the South, and he knew there were serious difficulties in the way of freeing his slaves. Slaves were needed in the South as a medium of exchange if for no other purpose. Much business was carried on through slave trading. No doubt Mr. Glover gave them in exchange for some of the material he used in erecting buildings. Part of the payment for his services may have been in slaves. If he refused to accept them his business would suffer.

Failing in her effort to free her husband's slaves, Mrs. Glover set about to do what she could with her pen. She was already a writer of some experience. Using a pen name, she now wrote articles opposing slavery and sent them to a Southern newspaper for publication. The articles must have been widely read, for a rival newspaper questioned in angry words "the identity of that . . . 'Yankee' who had come to Charleston to rob people of their property."

Long afterward Mrs. Eddy related to a friend some of her experiences in the South. She said that people were kind and hospitable except when slavery was mentioned. Her husband was somewhat outspoken in condemning the practice of slavery and was "once challenged to a duel by one who believed the Northerner would not fight." Mr. Glover, as the one challenged, had the right to choose the weapons and conditions. "He chose pistols 'toe to toe, and muzzle in the mouth.'" These severe conditions frightened the Southern gentleman, and he immediately withdrew his challenge. Mr. Glover's courage was not doubted again. Such experiences sound strange to us, but in early days duels were common. They were considered a gentleman's test of courage. A number of well-known men of history fought duels.

Shortly after their marriage Mr. Glover journeyed to Wilmington, North Carolina, to obtain materials for a church he had contracted to build in Haiti, and he took his wife with him. In June of the same year while still in Wilmington he died of yellow fever. Mary had prayed earnestly for his recovery, and the doctor said that her prayers lengthened her husband's life.

The slaves that Mr. Glover owned were now the property of his wife, and she freed them at once. Freeing them left her without means of support for herself and for her baby soon to be born. But Mary never counted the cost of doing right; and her father on whom she was now dependent agreed that the slaves should be set free.

CHAPTER 8

SOON after her husband's death Mrs. Glover returned to Tilton. For a long time she was not well, and it was feared that she might not live. In spite of the kindness of her friends and relatives her recovery was very slow. Her father especially devoted himself to her. He used to rock her in his arms to comfort her, and he tried to make the home as quiet as possible, even causing the road running past his house into Tilton to be covered with straw and tan bark to deaden the sound of horses' hoofs.

Her baby was born in September. He was a healthy little fellow. She named him George Washington Glover after his father. Mahala Sanborn, who often helped with the housework, was employed to nurse the mother and child. Mary had the care of her son very little during the years when she might have helped him grow into a more lovable child. Try as she would, she found herself not strong enough to care for the little fellow. He was left too much for his own good in the company of his faithful nurse. As long as Mahala remained in the household she took charge of him, and even after she returned home he was often with her. Whenever Abigail

54

visited the farm, as she did nearly every day, George was sent to the smithy to stay with Mahala. Mahala's father was a blacksmith. In early days blacksmiths had their shops at their homes and the shop was called the smithy. Abigail had a little son, Albert, about the same age as George. Albert was a delicate child, the opposite of his cheerful cousin. George was too rough for him, and it seemed best to keep them apart. Mahala was fond of George and kind to him; but she did not guide him as a wise mother would have done. Under her care he grew disobedient and self-willed.

In her later years Mrs. Eddy once told a friend the following story of her son's baby ways:

"When a widow & I sat rocking to sleep my baby boy as I gazed into his sweet face a big tear fell upon his soft cheek & wakened him. Reaching up his little hand to my face & half asleep he murmured 'mama not 'onesome Georgie is comp'ny. Georgie not s'eep' . . . his little hand fell & he slept on. Those tender words comforted me."

Mary's life was saddened by the death of her husband; yet she was cheerful and as active as her health would permit. She helped about the house, took care of her son whenever she was able, and entered into the church and social life of Tilton. A letter to her friend, Martha Rand, shows her effort to be active. It runs in this fashion:

"I have almost relinquished the hope of being at Concord this Summer to take lessons on the Piano. . . . Oh Mathy, how I wish we could be together this ensuing summer, get a school together or in some way manage it. We are busy now at the Maple Sugar business. . . ."

The postscript of the letter is a picture, a pleasing picture of a young mother and her child, for Mary wrote: "Please excuse this scrawl, George has been constantly at my elbow." In the picture the young mother is sitting at a desk on which lies an unfinished letter. At her elbow is a mischievous tot with little hand outstretched for the old ink-horn set in its walnut base or for the feather of the goosequill with which the gentle mother pens a letter to her friend.

When George was about four years old Mr. Baker retired from farm life and moved into Tilton, where he built a house next door to Abigail. He had become more prosperous through investing money in stocks and in workman's houses to rent. His new home was near the river. The murmur of the swift rapids could be heard in the stillness of morning as the rushing water turned the wheel of the cloth mill owned by Abigail's husband.

Not long after moving to town Mrs. Baker became very ill. Before the end of the following year, 1849, she passed away. Mary and her mother had been close companions during

56

Mary's twenty-eight years. Her mother's death deprived her of the companionship she had so long enjoyed and also emphasized the lack of a home of her own. The following year a stepmother came to her father's home, and there was no longer room for Mary and her son.

Having no home of her own and no means with which to establish one, Mary was forced to let her family make plans for her. Abigail, always generous, offered her sister a home, but the offer did not include George. Since there was no other way, Mary gave her unwilling consent to have him placed in charge of his former nurse, Mahala Sanborn, who had recently married and moved forty miles northward to North Groton.

Forty miles was nearly a day's stagecoach journey. It seemed a long distance in early days. With her son so far away, Mary knew she could not see him often.

She prayed earnestly for comfort and help, and the night before he was taken away scarcely left her knees. When morning came she packed his little garments, working bravely though tears filled her eyes.

She was sick much of the time while making her home with Abigail. Whenever strong enough she took part in the life of the town. She became a member of a debating society and sometimes spoke before its meetings. She was also active in church and Sunday school work. Her simple needs were supplied with money earned by writing and also serving as substitute teacher in the absence of regular teachers in the New Hampshire Conference Seminary. This Seminary was first built in 1845, just across the Winnepesaukee River in Northfield. The subjects taught in the school at that time were English, Moral and Intellectual Science, Natural Science, Mathematics, Latin, Greek, French, and Italian.

The principal of the seminary considered Mary an excellent teacher and urged her to open a school of her own. Later she did open an "Infants' School," to experiment with new ways of teaching. Infants' schools were much like kindergartens of the present. They were unlike other schools of early days.

58

Children who attended them were treated with kindness and encouraged to have an interest in learning. Indiana had the first "Infants' School," and from this beginning quite a number sprang up in various places. Most of them, including Mary's, had short lives. People feared the children would not learn if treated with too much kindness, and they were not willing to pay for such schooling.

As in former years Mary spent much of her time writing. A number of her poems and articles were printed in newspapers and magazines, and for some of them she received pay. One story was entitled, "Emma Clinton, or a Tale of the Frontiers." It was published in the *I. O. O. F. Covenant*.

Living with her sister was not wholly pleasant for Mary. Both sisters were ill much of the time. Although they always loved each other dearly, they sometimes had differences. Once at a party in her home Abigail became quite angry because Mary spoke against slavery and against the selection of Franklin Pierce for President of the United States. Mary did not favor Mr. Pierce because he was willing to permit slavery to continue. Abigail felt that her sister should support him because he was a native of New Hampshire and also a friend of the family. But Mary was an independent thinker. She was never afraid to speak and work for what she thought was right and against what she thought was wrong.

CHAPTER 9

AS years passed by, Mary became more and more lonely for her son. She longed to have a home of her own where she could watch him grow and have the comfort of his presence. To provide a home for him she married again. Her second husband was Dr. Daniel Patterson, a dentist. Mary hoped very much that she might have her child with her in her new home, but when the time came his stepfather refused to allow little George to live with his mother.

The first two years after their marriage, Dr. and Mrs. Patterson lived in Franklin, a fast-growing village a few miles west of Tilton. Here Dr. Patterson owned a cottage with a pasture around it where he kept his cow and the horse he drove on his professional rounds from village to village.

Their next home was in North Groton, a village in the foothills of the White Mountains, where George Glover still lived with his former nurse and her husband. The North Groton home was a farm of one hundred acres with a sawmill on it. One thousand dollars were borrowed from Mary's sister, Martha, to make a payment on the property.

The farm was beautifully located. Two huge blue mountains towering in hazy outline over the lower ranges formed a background for the farm and village homes in the foothills. During winter months woodsmen cut trees among the hills and sent them tumbling downstream to the many little sawmills in the valley. A heavy growth of pine, oak, and balsam covered the hillsides.

Mary loved nature and found inspiration in its beauty and grandeur. We may be sure that many verses from the Bible came to her mind as she looked from her window or the porch on sunny days to the hills and mountains beyond. No doubt she reverently repeated the words of the Psalmist, "I

61

will lift up mine eyes unto the hills, from whence cometh my help."

The house was a story-and-a-half building, made of wood and unpainted. Among White Mountain folk it was considered a mark of distinction to own a two-story house. Well-known people generally had houses of more than one story. An author who has written interesting stories about New Hampshire tells of one father who felt that the higher education he gave his daughter was wasted because she married a man who could give her only a one-story house.

From the outside Mary's house was like those of her neighbors, but inside it was different. She was a good housekeeper, and wherever she lived her home was neat and attractive. She had some good furniture, lovely pieces of walnut and mahogany, better than generally found in country homes of early days. Furniture was very expensive at that time; much of it was still brought over from England. Mary also had bits of silver service and some books and pictures. Some of the things had been her mother's. Arranged, as they were, with her good taste, the furnishings set her home apart from those of her neighbors.

Mary's husband was away much of the time. During his absence her only companion was a little blind girl, Myra Smith. Myra had come to the door one day looking for work, and Mary took her in. She kept the house neat and orderly and

62

waited on her mistress, cooking her meals and making her comfortable.

Myra's little sister, then ten years old, often visited her. Years afterward she wrote, "My blind sister . . . worked for Mrs. Patterson, consequently I was at the house two or three times each week. She was ill nearly all the time and would lie in bed, with a book for her constant companion but when I came up to the bedside she would lay aside her book and pat me on the hand and say, 'Oh you dear little girl. You are worth your weight in gold. I wish you were mine.' . . . One of the  greatest pleasures of the children was to carry in the earliest berries and wild flowers to the 'poor sick lady.' "

Mary was sick much of the time while in North Groton. Whenever strong enough she attended church, the Congregational Church, as she had in Concord and Tilton. She was friendly with her neighbors and visited with them when she could. But most of the time she was sick and had to remain at home, and often in bed. She spent long hours reading the Bible and studying a big doctor's book in hope of finding relief from suffering.

She was so earnest in her study of the Bible that many of her neighbors came to think of her as having spiritual power. Sometimes she was asked to pray for others. Once a blind babe was brought to her for help. As she looked at the little one, Mary's heart filled with love and pity. She remembered the words of Jesus, "Suffer the little children to come unto me, and forbid them not."

"Who," she asked herself, "has forbidden this little one, who is leading it into the way of blindness?"

Then she lifted her thought to God in prayer. When the mother again looked at her child, the eyes were healed.

How grateful Mary must have been for this healing! From early childhood she had faith in God's power to heal. We have seen how she was once healed of a fever through prayer. Her mother used to say to her, "God is able to raise you up from sickness." Mary believed her mother's words. She often recalled those words in later years in connection with the Scriptural passage, "And these signs shall follow them that believe; . . . they shall lay hands on the sick, and they shall recover." She wondered why the power to heal the sick through prayer had been lost. For several centuries after the crucifixion, Christians healed the sick as Christ Jesus and his disciples had done. Why do not Christians of today heal the sick as they did long ago? she questioned. Questions such as this were preparing

64

her thought for the discovery of Christian Science through which Christian healing is made practical for all time.

During the early part of her life in North Groton, Mary saw her son more often than formerly. He loved to be with her. He used to sit beside her as she lay in bed. She would talk with him and help him with his lessons. At length his foster parents moved away from North Groton to Minnesota, a distance of fifteen hundred miles, taking George with them. Several years after going to Minnesota he joined the Union Army to fight in the Civil War, which was beginning. This war was fought between the northern and southern states. It resulted in the emancipation of slaves and also in binding the states into a Union from which no state was permitted to withdraw.

Mary heard from her son while he was in the army, but she did not see him again until he was thirty-four. Later, when she was living in Boston, he brought his family from the West, where he was living, to visit her. She was a loving mother. She gave him money to start in business and to educate his children. Later, she provided a trust fund for him and his family. Mary Baker Glover, her granddaughter and namesake, became a Christian Scientist. When a child she was healed of crossed eyes by her grandmother. Long afterward she wrote of her healing as follows:

"When . . . I was three years old, my father went to visit his mother at Boston. At that time my eyes were . . . crossed, and during his visit he told grandmother about them. According to my father, grandmother said, 'You must be mistaken, George; her eyes are all right.'

"When he returned to our home . . . and during a conversation with my mother at my bedside while I was asleep, they awakened me and discovered that my eyes had become straightened. Mother has a picture of me taken before this incident, showing my eyes crossed. This healing was often told me by my father and mother, and is at this time verified by my mother, who is with me."

Some time after George went west with his foster parents, Dr. Patterson received an appointment to help with wartime work, and he went south. He did not return for a long time, for he strayed too near the Confederate lines and was taken prisoner. He wrote to Mary asking her to try to have him exchanged for some Southerner held in a northern prison. Exchanging prisoners was a common practice during the Civil War. Mary was not able to help her husband at once, because she was very ill. Later, when she was stronger, she borrowed money from his brother and journeyed to Washington with a letter from the Governor of New Hampshire to President Lincoln.

CHAPTER 10

MARY'S next home was in Lynn, Massachusetts, where her husband resumed his dental practice following his escape from the southern prison. This city was fourteen miles from Boston and had a population of 28,000 in 1870. It was a busy shoe manufacturing city. She later moved to Swampscott, a near-by town, where she received the remarkable healing that led to the discovery of Christian Science.

Although far from strong, Mary was in better health than formerly. Her improved health shortly before this time came about in an unusual way. Material remedies had not helped her, and her prayers had seemed to fail. But she did not lose faith in God. She used to say, "I know God can and will cure me, if only I could understand His way." Very weak and ill she finally visited a drugless healer whose work had been brought to her attention. She thought he must be practicing Christian healing, since he used no drugs. After a short visit with him her health was improved. Her faith in what she thought he practiced brought relief. But the healing was not permanent, and later she had a return of the same ailment.

With her improved health Mary was free to take an active part in the life of Lynn and Swampscott. She attended church regularly and also became a member of the Lynn Good Templar Society, an organization which worked for the cause of temperance. She sometimes gave talks before the meetings of this society. Long afterward its president spoke of her as a refined and intelligent woman. He said she had good manners and was generally quiet, always having something worth saying when she spoke.

She spent much of her time in writing. The Civil War was drawing to a close, and the thought of the time was seen in her writings, which showed a great love of country and an interest in freedom. Some of her poems were in the Lynn newspapers side by side with those of John Greenleaf Whittier, Oliver Wendell Holmes, and Phoebe Cary, all well-known American poets.

She also wrote news letters from Swampscott for publication in Lynn newspapers. These letters were chatty accounts of church affairs and parties, new homes and gardens. For a number of months a series of her articles with the modern title "Way-side Thoughts" appeared in a Portland, Maine, newspaper.

George Newhall, a milkman who belonged to the same church and temperance society she did, long afterward remem-

68

bered seeing her writing when he delivered the milk to her home in Swampscott. There was a fountain in the back yard walled up with granite. She used to sit there with a pad and pencil, sometimes writing and again looking into the water as if waiting for inspiration. When in deep thought she did not care to talk with others. Mr. Newhall also recalled hearing her read some of her writings before the temperance society.

So we find Mary just before the discovery of Christian Science, more happily situated than she had been for a number of years and leading a more active life. Then suddenly another trial came to her. One evening in February, 1866, she was seriously injured. The injury was the result of a fall on an icy street while on her way with some friends to a temperance meeting in Lynn. She was picked up unconscious and carried to a house near by. The doctor who attended her gave little hope for her recovery. Not until the following morning did she regain consciousness. Then she asked to be taken home. Although in great pain she was wrapped in furs and taken as carefully as possible to her home on Paradise Road, Swampscott. Some of her friends remained with her, and the pastor was called to bid her farewell. It seemed doubtful if she would recover.

In this hour of trial she turned to God as she always had done. Opening her Bible she read the story of the man with the palsy (Matthew 9:2). As she read, a new light dawned on her thought; never before had she been so certain of the presence and power of God. In that hour of need her heart was very close to the Father, whom she had loved and obeyed from a child, and she was instantly healed of the effects of the injury.

Her friends were delighted to see her restored; but they would not believe that God had healed her. A little girl of ten who visited her on that memorable day long afterward wrote:

"On the Sunday morning after Mrs. Eddy fell on the ice at Lynn, she sent for my mother. . . . My father got the horse, and we went down around noon. I can still see her as she lay on the couch. When we were leaving, I had gone into the hall when [she] said, 'When you come down the next time, I will be sitting up in the next room. I am going to walk in.' My mother said, 'Mary, what on earth are you talking about!' However, when we did go down that night (we had chicken for dinner, and mother carried down her supper), sure enough she was in the other room. And the doctor said she walked in."

George Newhall, the milkman already mentioned, also remembered the healing. The affair seemed stamped on his memory because he suffered so severely from the cold while driving several miles to inform the minister of the accident.

70

When he called with the milk as usual on the Sunday morning after the accident he was asked by some of Mary's friends to drive to Marblehead to tell the minister of her condition. There were no busses or street cars at that time nor any telephones to speed messages. Although the temperature was below zero Mr. Newhall kindly consented to go. He made the trip of several miles with his slow horse and business sleigh and was so nearly frozen that he could scarcely speak for some time after his return.

Long afterward, Mr. Newhall wrote down his recollections of these days. "Three or four mornings after, upon calling at the house," he relates, "Mrs. Millet informed me that a great change for the better had come over Mrs. Patterson. The evening before, to use Mrs. Patterson's own words, she says, 'I am going to walk.' Those present thought her mind wandering. She immediately pushed herself unaided to the side of the bed, placed her feet on the floor and walked to the side of the room and sat in a chair. Then she says, 'This is all through prayer,' it being the first time she had moved her legs without help since her injury. . . . The circumstances of which I have written are as fresh and clear in my memory as when they occurred."

Mary could not at first explain what had happened. The remarkable healing was to her what the falling apple was to

Newton. Others before him had seen apples fall and no doubt had wondered what made them fall. But he looked beyond the falling apple and discovered the rule which governs all material objects. This rule or law he named gravitation. Her healing proved to Mary that there is a rule of Christian healing. As she thought about her experience she decided that she must discover this rule and give her discovery to the world in order that mankind might always know how to heal the sick through prayer as Christ Jesus and the early Christians had done.

Mary was alone in her search for the rule of Christian healing. Her friends did not understand her desire to spend all her time studying the Bible and seeking to learn the way of spiritual healing. Her husband was not interested in Christian healing. His way was material, and he deserted her. Her brothers and sisters refused to give serious thought to her work.

After Mary was left alone, Abigail kindly offered to build her a house near her own and to give her an income so that she could spend all her time writing. With the offer was the condition that Mary return to her former church and be content with the religion of her family. Mary could have only one answer to this offer. She was doing God's work, and she would not turn back. Her lifework was to restore Christian healing to mankind. The work was already begun, and she knew she would carry it through to its completion.

72

CHAPTER 11

MARY was faithful in her effort to discover the rule of Christian healing. For several years after her healing from the effects of the fall on the ice, she spent nearly all  her time studying the Bible. Her hours were spent thinking about the message of the Bible and practicing Christian healing. Before offering the Christian Science textbook to the world she proved step by step that her discovery was from God.

The proof of her discovery lay in healing, even as did the Master's. When John sent to him questioning his Messiahship, Christ Jesus replied, "Go . . . tell John what things ye have seen and heard; how that the blind see, the lame walk, the lepers are cleansed, the deaf hear, the dead are raised, to the poor the gospel is preached" (Luke 7:22). Jesus intended this message to prove that he was the Messiah. Mary likewise proved that she was doing God's work by healing the sick and performing many wonderful works.

At first, in a number of instances, she asked people to permit her to heal them. Only in this way could she obtain patients and prove the truth of her discovery. One of her first patients was a child, Dorr Phillips. Dorr was the son of some dear Quaker friends. He had a bone felon on his finger. He was in pain and unable to attend school.

"Dorr, will you let me heal that felon?" she asked.

"Yes, indeed . . . , if you can do it," replied the lad.

"Will you promise not to do anything for it or let any one else, if I undertake to cure it?"

"Yes, I promise, and I will keep my word," said Dorr Phillips.

Then she told him not to look at the finger or talk about it, and she promised to pray for him. Dorr was obedient and was healed. "The boy actually forgot the felon and when his attention was called to the finger it was found to be well."

Another friend whom she healed was Mrs. Winslow. Mrs. Winslow had been confined to a wheel chair for sixteen years and was unable to walk. Her husband told Mary he would believe in divine healing and would even be willing to pay as much as one thousand dollars if she could heal his wife. Mary cried, "Why don't you understand that God will do the work if Mrs. Winslow will let Him?" However, she refused to accept the money. The proof of God's power to heal was the only reward she asked. Through her prayer Mrs. Winslow was healed and able to walk again for the first time in many years.

Sometimes Mary healed the sick by the wayside as in the case of a crippled man whom she happened to pass one day. He was sitting on the walk not far from where she was rooming in Lynn. His body was so out of shape that his knees touched his chin. Stepping to his side she said gently, "God loves you." In an instant the man stood up and walked. Mrs. Lucy Allen, who was watching from her window, saw this take place. Later the man came to her door and asked about the "angel" who had brought about the healing.

On Boston Common, a public park in the midst of the city, she once passed a cripple who had used a wheel chair for a number of years. Each pleasant morning a special policeman wheeled him to the park for an outing. As she passed by, Mary noticed his condition and stopped to speak to him. She told him he was God's perfect child and made other statements of truth. He said he felt better after talking with her, and he looked for her to come again. After several days she *did* pass that way once more. Again she stopped and spoke to him. This time he was made well. He had been so out of shape that he could not brush a fly from his face, but with his healing he regained full use of his hands and became a fine penman. He had been dependent on others, but now he was able to earn his own living.

75

One time an insane man wandered into the house in Lynn where Mary was rooming, frightening the landlady and her daughter. The daughter ran away, while her mother called Mrs. Eddy. When she entered the room the sick man picked up a chair to strike her. She stood looking at him fearlessly, and he became calm at once. Dropping the chair he fell to his knees. She spoke to him gently, telling him to go in peace. The man was healed from that hour. Long afterward he called on her at her home in Boston and expressed gratitude for the healing.

The healings related above are only a few of the many wonderful cures she performed. A full account of these and many others may be found in the stories of her life written for adults and published by The Christian Science Publishing Society in Boston, Massachusetts.

The summer after her healing Mary visited Abigail and other relatives and friends in Tilton and Concord. She longed to see her dear ones and to tell them the good news of salvation through Christian Science. There was need of healing among them. Both George and Abigail were very ill. Mary had long talks with them, telling them about her discovery and of the power of God to heal. But they were not ready for her message. However, she performed one cure during her visit. On arriving at the home of her sister Martha, she found her niece Ellen

76

Pilsbury seriously ill. Mary sat with her a few moments, and the girl was healed. The healing came at once, and Ellen was able to accompany her aunt to Taunton, a distance of about one hundred miles.

It would seem that Ellen's healing might have made other members of the family stop and think and perhaps accept Christian Science; but such was not the case. In spite of this wonderful proof, they refused to give serious thought to Mary's discovery. In time even Ellen herself came to laugh at Christian Science. She became angry when reminded that her aunt had healed her. She was influenced by the unbelief of her friends and relatives, who refused to believe that she had been healed through prayer. In later years two of her relatives told of the experience.

CHAPTER 12

AS we have seen, the first step in establishing Christian Science was healing the sick. Further important steps were writing the textbook and organizing the church with all its activities.

From the first, Mary realized that a textbook was needed to place in the hands of her students so that they might study the lessons she taught them. Soon after her healing she began writing explanations of Bible verses and stories. She also wrote thoughts of truth which came to her.

From 1867 until 1875 a manuscript entitled "The Science of Man" was in friendly circulation. This means that although the manuscript was not published until 1876, friends and students had the opportunity of reading and studying it as early as 1867. When printed, the material covered twenty-four pages. In 1881 it was added as the chapter entitled "Recapitulation" in the Christian Science textbook, "Science and Health with Key to the Scriptures."

This textbook was first published in 1875, nine years after the remarkable healing which marked the discovery of Christian Science. These nine years were spent studying and writing, and practicing Christian healing. For two and one half years Mary worked all the time, seven days a week, writing the textbook. In the fall of 1874 it was in the printer's hands, and in 1875 it was published. Changes were made from time to time to make its meaning clearer.

Mary's first student was Hiram Crafts, a shoemaker of Lynn and Taunton, Massachusetts. At that time he was employed in a shoe factory in Lynn. He sat next to her at the boarding-house table in the home of Mr. and Mrs. Clark, with whom she boarded more than once during the time she was searching for the rule of Christian healing.

Mr. Crafts was interested in her discovery, and she taught him Christian Science. Before long he gave up factory work and returned to his home in East Stoughton, Massachusetts, where he engaged in the practice of Christian healing. He advertised that he would refund the money paid for treatment if he failed to heal a case after being given a fair trial. One of his first patients was promptly healed of a serious illness. Her testimony appearing in a newspaper brought many patients to his door.

For a while Mary lived in East Stoughton and later on in Taunton with Mr. Crafts and his wife, spending her time in writing and helping him with his work. The success of her first student was very important to the growth of Christian

Science. It proved that her system is scientific, which means that it is based on a definite rule and can be taught to others.

In the beginning only a few sought teaching in Christian Science. In time the number increased so rapidly that it was necessary to establish a college to provide for their teaching. The college was called the "Massachusetts Metaphysical College" and was located in Boston. For nine years students poured into this college. A few of the classes were taught by students, but Mary did most of the teaching herself.

She gave sermons or lectures to help acquaint people with Christian Science. Often large crowds gathered to hear her speak. She had some experience in lecturing during her earlier years. Her lectures on Christian Science were more than ordinary talks. They were wonderful words of truth telling about the power of God and of His loving-kindness. Many times healings occurred among those who attended her lectures.

The janitor of one of the halls in Boston where she preached once brought his little daughter to hear the sermon. The child had been ill for a long time. She was too weak to walk to a seat in the hall, and her father had to carry her in. After the service, when leaving the hall, Mrs. Eddy noticed the sick child. She talked with her, and the girl listened and was healed. Soon she had forgotten that she ever was sick.

Mr. Henry A. Littlefield was one of a number who were

healed in Hawthorne Hall in Boston, where Mrs. Eddy held services for a time. He was unable to walk and had to be carried in on a cot. He was so ill that he could not bear the touch of bedding on his body. Mrs. Eddy noticed him, and on the way out after the service she stopped to speak to him. Mr. Littlefield afterward related, "When she came to me and shook my hand and spoke to me, I felt the healing and responded by telling her that I was healed. I walked out of the hall rejoicing, and that belief never made itself real to me again."

These and many other healings resulting from her sermons proved the truth of Christian Science and caused interest to grow rapidly. Soon there were Christian Scientists in many parts of the United States and in a number of foreign countries as well.

In the early days of Christian Science, many people doubted whether this religion would continue to prosper. Mary never doubted for a moment, nor did her faithful followers. She was certain that she would have a church, and that it would fulfill its mission to "reinstate primitive Christianity and its lost element of healing" (Manual of The Mother Church, p. 17).

The following story illustrates her faith in the future of Christian Science:

Once she and George Clark, son of the Clarks of Lynn with whom she boarded, went to Boston to consult a publisher about books they had written. George's book was a seafaring tale for boys, while Mary's was on the subject of Christian healing. The publisher accepted the tale for boys, but refused the religious writing, saying it would not sell.

On the return journey from Boston, she talked to George about his book. She encouraged him and praised his work, but did not mention her own. As they walked along the streets of Lynn, she suddenly caught his arm, " 'Stop, George,' she cried. 'Do you see that church? I shall have a church of my own some day.' "

The first step toward organizing a church was taken in 1875 when eight of her students together pledged the sum of ten dollars a week to pay the expenses of weekly services. Four years later the Church of Christ, Scientist, was organized in Boston. The work had been carried from Lynn into the larger city in 1878.

CHAPTER 13

THE little time that Mary took for recreation during those busy years was sometimes spent with children, for she loved to be with them. She lived in a number of different places during this time, but wherever she lived she found friends among the children of the household or neighborhood.

One of her difficulties at first was the lack of a suitable place in which to live. In a letter written before Science and Health was finished she speaks of having "no home to rest in" and "one room only to work in." She had very little money, scarcely enough to pay for her board and room. She could not afford to buy or rent a house; so she was forced to live in cheap boarding-houses and with families not used to the comforts she had enjoyed. Sometimes her room was so cold that she had to stop writing and go to the kitchen to warm her hands over the cook stove. Often she lacked proper food. She could easily have earned enough through her writing to support herself in comfort, but she chose to use her talents in restoring Christian healing to mankind.

Her many little friends delighted her. Sometimes they

would call on her to read with her or to talk with her. Some-times she would go with them for long walks hunting wild flowers or strolling down winding paths to the seashore.

One of her favorite walks was along the shore of the Atlantic Ocean to Red Rock, a lovely spot near Lynn. Red  Rock at that time was a quiet place at the end of a farm where there was no boulevard, but pasture land running down to the water. It is said that in the shelter of this huge rock, watching the waves dash against the shore, she thought of one of her beautiful poems entitled, "Christ My Refuge." This familiar poem ends:

> "My prayer, some daily good to do
> To Thine, for Thee;
> An offering pure of Love, whereto
> God leadeth me."
>
> (Poems by Mary Baker Eddy, p. 13.)

One little friend, with whom she spent some of these mo-ments taken for recreation, long afterward said of her:

"I loved her. . . . She was beautiful and had a good influ-ence over me. . . . We talked and read together and took long

84

walks in the country. . . . Her manners seemed to me so beautiful that I imitated her in everything."

Another little friend, already mentioned as the girl of ten who visited her on the day of her remarkable healing, wrote in later years that she remembered Mary well. She spoke of her as slender, with very bright eyes, and added, "She wore her hair with curls on each side of her head; there were two on each side, I think. She used to like to have me comb her curls, and I had a round stick on which I used to curl them."

Another child in her later years told of meeting her one summer when Mary was staying in Barre, Vermont. She spoke of the meeting as one of the loveliest and most distinct memories of her childhood.

Her father was a religious man but unfriendly to Christian Science and to its Discoverer. His criticism made the child curious to see Mary. One day when walking with two little friends she led the way straight to the house where Mary was staying. She lay in the hammock resting; but when she saw the children she arose to greet them. To use the little girl's own words:

"As she approached us, I was conscious of the beautiful

picture she made. The expression in her eyes and the lovely smile she gave us are unforgettable. She talked to us very kindly, asked our names, and talked about the flowers which were growing in the yard. Finally, she picked a small bouquet for each of us, and we went home.''

She always delighted to heal children, and she healed quite a number of them. One was a little boy named Stanley, a self-willed, bad-tempered child. He was very ill when brought to her, and his mother feared it was too late to save him. Mary knew that it is never too late to call on God for help and to apply His law. She took the sick child from his mother and laid him on a bed. Then she turned to God in prayer. Before long the little fellow sat up and began repeating willfully, ''I is tick; I is tick.'' Mary replied, ''You are not sick, and you are a good boy.'' He rallied at once and was soon well. His mother reported later that he had been cured of ill temper as well as of brain fever from which he suffered, for his disposition was greatly improved.

Near her home on Columbus Avenue, Boston, there lived a dear little girl who had never walked. Mary used to watch her from the window. Once she missed the child for several days and stopped at the neighbor's door to ask about her. The mother informed her that her daughter had been very ill and had just died. Mary asked to be left alone with her. The mother felt certain nothing could be done for her little one; however, she consented to leave her alone with her friend.

As the door closed on the mother, Mary took the lifeless body in her arms and began to pray. Her heart was so filled with truth and love she forgot the sick child until she sat up and asked for her mother. When her mother came, she jumped down from Mary's lap and ran to meet her. She had never walked before. The treatment raised her from the dead and fully made her well so that she could walk, run, and play like other children.

CHAPTER 14

AFTER living for several years in boarding houses and with friends and students, Mary at length bought a home of her own on Broad Street in Lynn. At that time her income was not large enough to permit her to use the entire house for herself. Therefore she rented all but the downstairs parlor and an attic bedroom in which she spent many hours studying and writing. The bedroom was small and plainly furnished, with only a skylight for a window. On the wall hung a motto, the First Commandment, "Thou shalt have no other gods before me" (Exodus 20). She has named this commandment her favorite text.

Not long after she moved into her new home, the Christian Science textbook, "Science and Health with Key to the Scriptures," was published. Part of the work on the book was done in the little attic room. In this little room the name for her book came to her thought, a name as remarkable as the book itself. She prayed earnestly for the right title; and one starlit night the words "Science and Health" came to her waiting thought. She did not know until some

time later that the phrase, "knowledge of salvation," is rendered "Science and Health" in one translation of the Bible. The books of the Bible were written long ago. Greek and Hebrew were the languages commonly used then.

Mary was glad to have a home of her own, a quiet place in which to write and study and receive her students and patients. Her students were as happy over the new home as their teacher. They spent many hours making it attractive, caring for the little plot of grass and filling the balcony with calla lilies, which she liked very much. Often groups of her students gathered with her in the parlor to talk or to sing. Especially on Sunday evenings they used to sing hymns together.

Mrs. Eddy loved to sing and frequently gained help from hymns. She liked to sing old familiar tunes such as "Annie Laurie" and "Comin' thro' the Rye." Often at the twilight hour she would join her sweet voice with others of her household in singing songs they all loved. She enjoyed her friends and loved to be with them and to share their joys and sorrows; but her thought was not on material things. Her talk was of spiritual things rather than of material. A man who knew her well said that in talking with her, one was led to voice only good and not evil.

While living in her home in Lynn she acted as a friend to a little girl from Russia whose name was Nadia Swartz. Many years later the Russian girl still remembered her kindness. Nadia had been in America only a short time when she met Mrs. Eddy. She was living with an aunt whose back door was opposite the back of the Broad Street home. The child was lonely and unhappy. Her aunt was unkind to her, and she knew no English except the few words, "I speak no English." One

90

day, when she was hanging up baby clothes in the back yard and singing a little Russian song as she worked, Mrs. Eddy called to her. This meeting was the beginning of a pleasant friendship which lasted until Nadia moved away from Lynn.

Nadia's aunt did not understand Mrs. Eddy and her work and warned the child against her. But Nadia felt the depth of her affection from the first. Whenever her aunt was away she would go to the back door of Mrs. Eddy's home and knock. To use her own words: "Often Mrs. Eddy would say, 'I am busy child, come back some other time.' . . . On Saturdays I was left alone to do the work. As soon as my work was done I would take my little dictionary and go to see Mrs. Eddy. There was a little stool by her chair on which I would sit . . . while she was reading and writing. I do not recall a time when she was not doing one or the other."

Sometimes Mrs. Eddy sent Nadia on errands, first teaching her the English words needed. Once, after teaching her to say, "Please Mrs. Eddy's leg of lamb," she sent her to the butcher shop. On her way she passed some schoolmates who were looking at pictures of themselves taken by a traveling photographer. The pictures were small and printed in strips and were called, "Ping-pong." Nadia was so interested in the pictures that she forgot the English words. To the amusement of the shopkeeper she said, "Mrs. Eddy's ping-pong."

Mrs. Eddy begged her to go back and try again; but Nadia was ashamed and would not go back. Later with the help of her little Russian dictionary she wrote a note to her friend telling her how sorry she was and slipped it under the door. The next day when again hanging up clothes in the yard, she heard Mrs. Eddy call. In Nadia's words:

"She kissed me on my forehead, stroked my hair and said she understood just how I felt about the mistake . . . and said that we must learn by our mistakes; that the stumbling blocks must be made into stepping stones."

Once Mrs. Eddy gave Nadia money to buy a white shirt-waist such as her schoolmates were wearing and taught her the words needed to buy it. She understood the child's desire to dress like her friends. This little act of kindness was just like Mrs. Eddy. She seemed to understand the needs of those about her, and she was always doing kind deeds.

Before leaving Lynn, Nadia called on her friend to bid her good-by. Mrs. Eddy put her arms around her and told her she would be proud of her some day. Mrs. Eddy gave the child a picture of herself and also a book of poems written by a young student whose parents were born in Russia.

Many years later Nadia journeyed to Pleasant View in Concord, where Mrs. Eddy then lived, to see her and to hear her speak to a large number of her followers who had gathered

92

at her home. Mrs. Eddy remembered her well and kissed her on the forehead as of old. She told her how pleased she was with her English. In Nadia's words:

"I shall never forget the tenderness with which Mrs. Eddy took me in her arms and held me close for a moment. . . .

"I watched her on her balcony while she addressed a tremendous large group. I was thrilled beyond expression. . . . She wore a very small bonnet, her beautiful snow-white hair showing, with an ermine cape on her shoulders, no whiter than her beautiful hair."

CHAPTER 15

WE have seen how deep an affection Mrs. Eddy had for children. She understood them and loved them, and she showed her love for them in many ways. One of her gifts to children of all time is the Christian Science Sunday School. In the Sunday school, children learn to know and love the Bible and to find therein the way to be happy, healthy, and good. They learn how to solve their own problems and how to help others.

The following is the last stanza of a poem which Mrs. Eddy wrote for the Sunday school children:

> "Temper every trembling footfall,
>   Till they gain at last—
> Safe in Science, bright with glory—
>   Just the way Thou hast:
> Then, O tender Love and wisdom,
>   Crown the lives thus blest
> With the guerdon of Thy bosom,
>   Whereon they may rest!"

(Poems by Mary Baker Eddy, pp. 43, 44.)

The Christian Science Sunday School was first organized on October 25, 1885, ten years after the publication of the

Christian Science textbook, "Science and Health with Key to the Scriptures." It was not entirely forgotten during these ten years. Asa Gilbert Eddy conducted a Sunday school in 1881. Referring to this beginning, Mrs. Eddy speaks of him as the first organizer of the Sunday school. There are no records telling how this first Sunday school was conducted. "Probably it was informal, and did not last long. Probably, also, it was for adults, rather than for children."

Mr. Eddy was a faithful student of Christian Science. He came to Mary for healing and when restored to health entered one of her classes. Soon he became a Christian Science practitioner. He was the first to place the name, "Christian Scientist," over his door. Mr. Eddy was a man of strong character. His great goodness won Mary's affection, and they were married on New Year's Day, 1877. Although he lived only a few years after their marriage, he was of great help to Mrs. Eddy in establishing Christian Science.

A mention of the Sunday school is made in the written story of one of Mrs. Eddy's early students. It seems that several years before the organization of the Sunday school in 1885 a number of Mrs. Eddy's students were gathered together in her parlor one Sunday evening, talking and singing hymns as they often did. After the singing, little Warren Choate, the five-year-old son of a student, climbed to Mrs. Eddy's lap. She put her arms around him affectionately and told him how well he had behaved that afternoon during the service. Then she added, "Well, we must have a Sunday school, Warren. You shall be the first pupil."

The following day she sent for him to come to her room. He dressed carefully before going, making sure his hands and face were clean and his hair well brushed. While he was dressing he reminded his mother frequently, "Mrs. Eddy is very fussy." Warren knew that Mrs. Eddy was not patient with a speck of dirt. She expected everyone about her to be as neat and clean as she always was.

During that week she worked with the child several times, teaching him a piece to speak before the audience the following Sunday. When Sunday came he dressed in his best for the occasion, wearing a white suit with wide collar and cuffs and a blue sash. Mrs. Eddy was well dressed as usual and wore a rose in her hair to please her little friend.

As the service began, she took the lad by the hand and led him to the platform. She introduced him as a member of the Christian Science Sunday School who would speak a piece. He stepped forward and bowed gracefully as she had taught him. Then he began:

96

"For right is right, since God is God;
And right the day must win;
To doubt would be disloyalty,
To falter would be sin!"

(Frederick W. Faber)

These words are now in the Christian Science Hymnal, in Numbers 86 and 87.

At first the Sunday school was for adults as well as for children. The Sunday following its organization, seventy adults and children attended. From time to time changes were made in the Sunday school until Mrs. Eddy included rules for its conduct in The Mother Church Manual.

Mrs. Eddy remembered children in other ways as well as in the Sunday school. As early as 1886 *The Christian Science Journal,* then three years old, had a department for parents and children. At one time the *Christian Science Sentinel* had a department headed, "For the Children." This department had stories, book reviews, and poems especially for children and young people. It also had some articles on teaching Christian Science to children. Today, there are articles for young people in the *Sentinel.*

Children had a part in building the original Mother Church edifice. A group of children, called "Busy Bees," gave money to provide a room for Mrs. Eddy which was called the "Mother's Room." This room was built in the tower of The Mother

Church. The room was planned for Mrs. Eddy's use when visiting in Boston. She used it twice when she visited The Mother Church. The Busy Bees also furnished flowers for The Mother Church. After a time Mrs. Eddy asked the children to give up their organization and to use the money they earned mainly for their education.

Mrs. Eddy's followers, both younger and older, sometimes made plans to help with the work of establishing Christian

98

Science which she felt were not the best. She might let them have their experience, knowing that in time they would see that the only way to advance the work of Christian Science is through spiritual growth and healing. One such experience happened in 1887. A number of young Christian Scientists, aided by their elders, gave a fair to help pay for the land on which the original Mother Church edifice was to be built. They rented a hall and decorated it with Japanese fans and lanterns. Cakes, candy, fancywork, and all sorts of trinkets were sold in booths. Mrs. Eddy attended the fair with her son and his family, who had come from the West to visit her. She spoke to those in the hall and expressed her appreciation of the interest taken by the young people. The fair seemed a success, but in the end it was a failure, for all the money earned was lost through the dishonesty of one of the workers.

Children were remembered in the dedication of The Mother Church Extension. A special service was held for them at noon. They filled every seat in the body of the huge auditorium and took part in the singing and responsive reading just as their elders had done earlier in the day. Their happy voices kept perfect time with the great pipe organ. Their service was exactly like the other services held that day. The children understood it and enjoyed it as much as their parents. Christian Science is simple and easily understood by both children and adults.

99

CHAPTER 16

THE work of Christian Science was carried into Boston, Massachusetts, several years before Mrs. Eddy made that city her home. She continued living in her Broad Street home in Lynn, except for short periods of residence in Boston, until April, 1882, when she removed permanently from Lynn to Boston. From then until 1889 she lived at 569 Columbus Avenue, 571 Columbus Avenue, and 385 Commonwealth Avenue. During these years her time was spent in healing, teaching, preaching, and writing.

Interest in her religion was spreading rapidly, and the demands on her time were many. At length it seemed best for her to retire to a place where she could give more time to writing and planning for the establishment of the work of Christian Science. In 1889 she moved from Boston to Concord, New Hampshire, where she remained for nearly twenty years. Her new home was only a few miles from her birthplace. Memories of a happy childhood made the surroundings very dear to her; and when it seemed best to retire to a place where she could be free from the many demands made on her, she chose to make her home once more among her native hills.

Concord was far enough from Boston to give her some freedom from calls and yet near enough to permit her to watch over the growing movement. She watched it tenderly and eagerly as a wise mother watches the growth of her child. With special messengers sent between Boston and Concord many times each week she kept in close touch with the work. One of these messengers, then a young boy, speaks of her delicate beauty and her lovely smile as one of the most precious memories of his boyhood.

For some time she had been preparing her students to do more and more healing and teaching, and now a large number were fitted to do the work. Her students were becoming more capable of giving lectures and writing and doing other work necessary to advance Christian Science. From this time The Christian Science Board of Directors of The Mother Church took on more responsibility, as she was ever encouraging them to do. She was a wise spiritual Leader, and she urged her followers to turn to God and not to person. In seeking divine help they were fitting themselves to carry on the work of Christian Science and thus to bless the world.

There was still a great work to be done that only Mrs. Eddy could do. This task was the completion of the organization. Among the forward steps taken during her years in Concord were the building of The Mother Church, both the

101

original edifice and the Extension, the establishment of The Christian Science Publishing Society, the *Christian Science Quarterly,* the *Christian Science Sentinel,* and *The Herald of Christian Science,* German Edition. Before the publication of the *Christian Science Quarterly,* Mrs. Eddy preached in her church. Later on, services were conducted by ministers or by Mrs. Eddy's own students. Then, in 1895, Mrs. Eddy ordained the Bible and the Christian Science textbook as the only preachers, and the citations from these books, which made up the Lesson-Sermons for the Sunday services, were published in the *Quarterly.*

For three years after moving northward Mrs. Eddy lived at 62 North State Street, Concord, except for a short time when she resided in Roslindale, Massachusetts. During two of these  years she worked steadily on Science and Health, preparing it for an important edition in which she added about fifty pages and made a number of changes to make the meaning clearer.

While living in Boston she had begun the practice of taking afternoon drives, and she continued this practice in Concord. She loved to drive about over the hills and valleys, the scenes of her childhood. Often she drove to the outskirts of the city where she could see long distances. There she would halt her carriage and look out over the broad valley to the distant mountains as she did when a child. This was the view of her childhood home; and she longed for another home where she could again look out on her native hills.

A great change had come over the country around Concord since her childhood. It was no longer the rural scene of her youth, with broad fields of golden grain, orchards bright with ripening fruits, and flocks and herds on hillside and meadow. In common with all New England many of the farms had been left to run wild once more. Overrunning the land was a dense growth of fern and thistle, scrub oak and poplar. Mrs. Eddy pictures the loneliness of the scene around her childhood home in the following words: "Now the lone night-bird cries, the crow caws cautiously, and wandering winds sigh low requiems through dark pine groves" (Retrospection and Introspection, p. 4).

Many of the settlers who formerly lived on farms had become business men in the busy milling and factory towns that dot New England. Others had followed the trail of the covered wagon westward. Western soldiers who fought beside their New England comrades during the Civil War told inviting tales of the fertile land at home. The great stretches of

103

rich prairie land, with neither trees nor stones in the way of the plow, were tempting to New England farmers who were used to struggling with the heavy growth of trees and the many stones that covered their land. New roads as well as new railroad lines and canals made travel easier, so a great many farmers left their farms idle and their farmhouses empty and journeyed westward. Thus the rural population of New England became smaller. Bow had a population of 1,000 in Mrs. Eddy's childhood and only 780 one hundred years later.

At length Mrs. Eddy found a location for her new home. She bought a thirty-six-acre farm with a house which she had enlarged and made suitable for herself and her helpers. A number of faithful students were now living with her, serving their Leader and the Cause of Christian Science. They had been called from many parts of the Field. To receive such a call was a great honor. Mr. Calvin A. Frye, her first secretary, and Mrs. Laura E. Sargent, her companion, were members of the household for the longest periods. There were others equally faithful—secretaries, assistant secretaries, assistant housekeepers, and maids.

The home stood on Pleasant Street. It was a home of a pleasant view; and Pleasant View she named it. Around the house were smooth lawns and stately trees. To the back were flower gardens, pastures, and meadows. The dear little pond

104

at the back of the house was a gift of some students. A beautiful boat, also given by students, drifted peacefully on the still water. Soft mosses grew at the water's edge, and frogs sunned themselves on lily pads through the long summer hours. Pleasant View was a restful home, and Mrs. Eddy loved it.

In 1898 while still at Pleasant View she taught her last class. The class was composed of earnest students whom she invited to come to her for instruction. She said she was "glad to give to the world such men and women to demonstrate Christian Science."

Mrs. Eddy was a natural teacher, and she delighted to teach. She knew how to make her subject interesting and how to explain a point so that the lesson would not be forgotten. Sometimes she told an amusing story to help teach a lesson. The following story was told to point out the error of misrepresenting:

It seems that her father was in need of a carriage horse. He considered buying one from his neighbor, but hesitated, fearing the animal was too skittish. Said the neighbor, "Mr. Baker, you couldn't scare this horse, no matter what you did." Mr. Baker replied that the horse would probably jump if he said "boo." The owner offered to put it to a test. So they decided that Mr. Baker should hide behind a stump in the field, and when the owner rode by he was to jump out and say "boo." All went well until the horse reached the stump. Mr. Baker jumped out, threw up his hands and shouted "boo." The horse threw his rider and galloped madly across the field. The owner got up and brushed the dirt off his clothes. "Well, Mr. Baker," he said, "that was too big a 'boo' for such a small horse."

CHAPTER 17

MRS. EDDY always made good use of her time. Her days were carefully planned so that there would be time enough to do whatever needed to be done. She once said, "Just a little duty performed each hour and each day, and at length symmetrical unity." At six in the summer and seven in the winter she arose. Often she worked far into the night. Many hours of each day were given to study, prayer, and writing.

When she entered her study in the morning, she would open her Bible or Science and Health and read the first line or verse her eyes rested upon. Sometimes she would call to one or more of her household, "Come and hear what God said to me this morning." Then from the depths of her understanding of God she would read to them; and they would rejoice and be glad for the spiritual good in the message.

Sometimes she would walk through the many rooms of her house. Occasionally she would arrange a scarf, a bouquet, or an ornament on the whatnot, and at other times she would direct changes in the furnishings. Her main reason for the walk was one of friendliness. It was an opportunity to speak with

her helpers, the laundress, the cook, the secretaries, and the gardener. None were left out; and all looked forward to her coming. Her friendly jokes, kind words, and spiritual advice made her visit the bright spot of the day. They all loved her and felt the blessing of her presence.

Dinner at Pleasant View was at noon, and it always ended with homemade ice cream. Mrs. Eddy was very fond of ice cream, and the sound of the freezer grinding away in the kitchen could be heard through the house regularly each morning, telling that it was near dinnertime.

After dinner she went for a drive in her fine carriage drawn by two black horses. Mr. Frye often sat with the coachman in his box, and occasionally he drove. Since the daily drive was almost the only time for many years that she appeared in public, it became a matter of general interest. People used to stand by the roadside to watch her pass and to greet her. Little children often stopped their play  to wave. Sometimes she carried bags of oranges and candy with her to treat her little friends. Even to the end, on that cold December day when she was last seen riding out from her home, children waited by the roadside to wave to the "dear old lady," as many lovingly called her.

Mrs. Eddy often did little deeds of kindness. She was a busy woman; but she was never too busy to be loving and thoughtful of others. An example of her thoughtfulness is found in a story told by one who as a child was twice healed by Mrs. Eddy. This incident occurred while Mrs. Eddy lived at Pleasant View.

"One day . . . she asked the gardener to bring a basket of vegetables, carefully packed, to send on the train to one of her students who lived in an adjoining town . . . she sent the gardener to the basement for a generous piece of salt pork.

109

This she had carefully wrapped in paper and tied to the side of the handle so it would be held securely in the basket; she then slipped in a note expressing her pleasure at sending the vegetables from her own garden, and added: 'With the salt pork I think you have all the ingredients necessary for a good meal.' "

Mrs. Eddy was an honored resident of Concord, and well she might be. Her gifts to the city amounted to many thousands of dollars. She was always ready to give to worthy causes. The hard-surfaced road from Pleasant View to the city was one of her gifts to Concord. Another gift was the beautiful Christian Science church. For a number of years she made it a practice to supply the needy children of the city with stout shoes. The opening day of the Concord Fair was Children's Day, and children were admitted to the grounds free. On the same day, through Mrs. Eddy's kindness, each needy child received a pair of shoes. Many of the parents were also supplied with footwear.

Mrs. Eddy twice accepted an invitation to attend the Concord Fair. At this Fair the people from the surrounding country displayed their prize cattle, farm produce, and handiwork. Candy and toys were sold, and there were many different forms of entertainment. On one of these occasions, as an honored guest, Mrs. Eddy was given a special welcome. Thou-

110

sands waved their handkerchiefs to greet her and thousands made way for her carriage. After the talks, including one by the Governor of New Hampshire, attention was turned to amusements. The main attraction was a high-diving act. Mrs. Eddy asked to see this exhibition, so her carriage was driven to the side of the pool. The diver, dressed in red with a tail to represent Satan, was to dive from a high platform through a hoop of fire into a small pool of water. Mrs. Eddy said she was glad to see the performance, because it was an example of overcoming fear. The diver did well, diving gracefully downward through the fiery circle into the water far below and coming quickly to the surface. When out of the water he walked up to Mrs. Eddy's carriage, bowed low before her and then ran off. When he disappeared in the crowd Mrs. Eddy remarked humorously to some Christian Scientists who were with her, "I beheld Satan as lightning fall from heaven."

Mrs. Eddy seldom left Concord while she lived there. However, she kept in touch with her followers. Several times she visited her church in Boston. She also received many calls from individual students, as well as from others who were not her students. On several occasions she invited her followers to call in a body. About two hundred accepted her first invitation, given in 1895. She shook hands with all of them and talked with many. Two years later twenty-five hundred

Christian Scientists visited her on the day after the communion service in The Mother Church. The number was too large to be received indoors, so lemonade was served on the lawn after she spoke to them from the balcony. In 1901, she again permitted her students to gather at Pleasant View. Two years later, in 1903, nearly ten thousand Christian Scientists called at her home, where she addressed them from her balcony. Just before time for her to speak one of her secretaries entered the room, and she invited him to remain and hear her address through the open window. Long afterward he told what he remembered of that happy day in these words:

"She then called her maid to put on her wrap and bonnet. It was raining a little, but this ceased when she went out. A multitude of joyous, upturned faces greeted their dear Leader in a stillness indescribable. She started right in and delivered her brief address slowly and distinctly. I was afterwards informed that every word was heard, so clear was her enunciation. She returned to her room . . . , her face radiantly happy. The maid removed her wrap and bonnet and she sat down in her big chair, folded her hands, and said to me, 'Wasn't it a wonderful occasion?' Then she asked me, 'What are they doing?' I looked below and told her they were having silent prayer. 'We will pray, too,' she said. 'Now what are they doing?' she asked. 'They are singing your hymn "Shepherd," Mother.'"

112

After the crowd had gone she took her Bible and opened it with no particular place in mind. Her eyes rested upon the verse, "And the ransomed of the Lord shall return, . . . with songs . . . and gladness, and sorrow and sighing shall flee away." " 'See,' she said, 'how God is always with me. That verse I will add to my address.' "

CHAPTER 18

MRS. EDDY'S years spent in Concord were happy and fruitful. They were years set apart for giving. During this time she gave to children the following verses found in "Miscellaneous Writings" (p. 400), a book published while she lived at Pleasant View.

"MOTHER'S NEW YEAR GIFT TO THE LITTLE CHILDREN

"Father-Mother God,
    Loving me,—
Guard me when I sleep;
Guide my little feet
    Up to Thee.

"TO THE BIG CHILDREN

"Father-Mother good, lovingly
    Thee I seek,—
    Patient, meek,
In the way Thou hast,—
Be it slow or fast,
    Up to Thee."

On Sunday, January 26, 1908, she bade farewell to Pleasant View and Concord and journeyed to Chestnut Hill, a suburb of Boston, where she spent the remainder of her life.

114

Mrs. Eddy was now a famous person, and her movements were closely watched, especially by newspaper reporters. She wished to return to Boston with as little publicity as possible; therefore few except members of her household knew of her plan to remove to Chestnut Hill. On Sunday afternoon she went out for her drive as usual; but instead of returning to Pleasant View she drove to the railroad station, where a special train was waiting for her.

News of her going spread rapidly; and when she reached her new home reporters were waiting on the grounds. To avoid them Mrs. Eddy asked a member of her household to help her through the crowd. He was tall and strong, and picking her up in his arms he carried her into the house. She was in a merry mood and laughed like a child at the fun of being more clever than the newspapermen.

The new home was lovely. It was larger than the home at Pleasant View and better suited to the size of her household. It was well furnished and contained a number of costly ornaments, most of them gifts from students. Mrs. Eddy loved simplicity. Her private rooms at Chestnut Hill were made as nearly as possible a copy of her simple rooms at Pleasant View. Some of her furniture was moved from Concord; among these things was the whatnot of which she was fond. She enjoyed arranging its ornaments and would sometimes pause to do so

when she walked through the house visiting with members of her household.

One of the several reasons for Mrs. Eddy's move from Pleasant View to Chestnut Hill was to be near the headquarters of Christian Science during the establishment of *The Christian Science Monitor*. The *Monitor* was one of her greatest gifts to the world. She had long desired to publish a daily newspaper which would express the Christian Science point of view. Now the time had come to go forward with the plan.

There were a number of difficulties in the way of publishing a daily newspaper, and few, except Christian Scientists, felt that the paper would be a success. Even a few faithful Christian

116

Scientists urged Mrs. Eddy to change the name to one that would not point definitely to Christian Science. She refused; and time has proved that in this decision, as in all decisions connected with Christian Science, she was led of God. She knew that the paper would in time be recognized as one of the best newspapers ever published and would lead many to Truth. In her words, "The object of the *Monitor* is to injure no man, but to bless all mankind" (Miscellany, p. 353).

Through *The Christian Science Monitor* Mrs. Eddy once more showed her great love for children. The paper has several features of interest for both younger and older children. The first issue of the paper came out on Wednesday, November 25, preceding Thanksgiving Day in 1908.  Since that day thousands of children have read the stories, book reviews, and poems published especially for them.

About two years after the first issue of the *Monitor* Mrs. Eddy passed away. The date was December 3, 1910. She was nearly ninety years of age, but she did not seem old. To the end she was active and happy and still carrying on her great lifework.

Her lifework is blessing people of all races and nations, children and adults alike. Mrs. Eddy knew that children of all time would love Christian Science because it is simple and beautiful and easy to understand. She loved children for their faith, their purity, their joy, and their willingness to receive and practice the truth. She had confidence in them and expected them to be earnest, working Christian Scientists. She left a strong and stirring challenge to them in these words, "Ah, children, you are the bulwarks of freedom, the cement of society, the hope of our race!" (Pulpit and Press, p. 9.)

COPYRIGHT ACKNOWLEDGMENTS

119